The Wilderness Concept and the
Three Sisters Wilderness

Deschutes and Willamette National Forests, Oregon

Revised Edition

Les Joslin

Central Oregon Community College
Oregon State University

Wilderness Associates
Bend, Oregon

THE WILDERNESS CONCEPT AND THE THREE SISTERS WILDERNESS

Revised Edition

Les Joslin

For information address Wilderness Associates, P.O. Box 5822, Bend, Oregon 97708

Library of Congress Control Number: 00-090534

International Standard Book Number: 0-9647167-4-7

Printed and Bound in the United States of America by Maverick Publications, Inc. P.O. Box 5007, Bend, Oregon 97708 for Wilderness Associates P.O. Box 5822, Bend, Oregon 97708

The dedication of this little book is not as simple as it should be because there are so many to whom it should be dedicated.

This book, therefore, is dedicated to
Raymond R. Hatton, Ph.D.
Professor Emeritus of Geography,
Central Oregon Community College,
friend, mentor, colleague, and the first person
to introduce me to the
Three Sisters Wilderness;
the
Wilderness Management Professionals
of the Deschutes National Forest,
who, since 1990, have entrusted and honored me with
opportunities to serve in the Three Sisters Wilderness
and to develop a wilderness education program that I
sincerely hope has and will continue to meet their needs;
the
Wilderness Information Specialists,
volunteers and student interns who, since 1993, have
fully qualified for and served complete tours of duty at
the trailheads and on the trails of the Three Sisters Wilderness,
without whose dedicated service the program would not succeed
and
Jim Leep,
mounted wilderness ranger and packer who dedicated
a dozen summers to "caring for the land and serving people"
in the Three Sisters Wilderness.

Something will have gone out of us as a people
if we ever let the remaining wilderness be destroyed....

—Wallace Stegner

Distinctive signs mark Three Sisters Wilderness boundaries.

CONTENTS

PREFACE

There are many excellent hiking and backpacking guides to the Three Sisters Wilderness, but this is not one of them. This book, instead, is a short guide to a more profound wilderness experience. It is a guide to an understanding of the Three Sisters Wilderness *as wilderness*—to its natural and cultural history, and to the philosophical, legal, and management concepts that combine to keep it a wilderness.

"Wilderness" is a word and an idea that Americans are still learning, and that means different things to different people. Chapter One examines the evolution and expression of the meaning given the word by the Wilderness Act of 1964 and the National Wilderness Preservation System, generally, and the Three Sisters Wilderness, particularly. One who would read a more comprehensive work on wilderness as a concept would do well to turn to Roderick Nash's classic, *Wilderness and the American Mind*, and then read and consider current commentaries on and critiques of the concept beyond the scope of this book.

Chapter Two summarizes the natural and cultural history of the Three Sisters Wilderness. This summary introduces the wilderness that is being preserved and the human influences on that wilderness before and—to a certain extent—after it was set aside by Congress to be preserved. This is the only such summary published to date. This chapter is best read—or studied—with the current edition of Al Cardwell's *Three Sisters Wilderness Map* as a ready reference.

Chapter Three summarizes the administrative and stewardship efforts that add up to the art and science of wilderness management, and relates the principles and practices of wilderness management to the effort to keep the Three Sisters Wilderness wild. There is, of course, much more to wilderness management in general, and to management of the Three Sisters Wilderness in particular, than can be included in this brief chapter. The standard work on wilderness management is John C. Hendee's and Chad P. Dawson's *Wilderness Management: Stewardship and Protection of Resources and Values*.

This little book claims no original discovery. Rather, it contributes an ordered introduction to its subject based on research of available information and on years of personal experience and observation. It began as a textbook for a short course at Central Oregon Community College, which contributed a small Program for Excellence in Teaching (PET) grant to help support its development, and for the general reader who is interested in the Three Sisters Wilderness and its management. Since 2002, it's also been one of the three textbooks for the Oregon State University wilderness management course the author teaches through that university's Extended Campus. It was revised slightly late in 2004, the 40th anniversary of the passage of the Wilderness Act of 1964 and the establishment of the National Wilderness Preservation System—and of the designation of the Three Sisters Wilderness as an original unit of that System—to reflect the changes of the past four years.

The colleagues who and works that contributed to this effort are recognized in the acknowledgments, bibliography, and credits.

Les Joslin
Bend, Oregon
Winter, 2005

Chapter One

THE WILDERNESS CONCEPT
AND THE GEOGRAPHY OF HOPE

The Three Sisters and Broken Top dominate the Cascade Range in Central Oregon. This unique, closely-grouped cluster of volcanic peaks and surrounding Deschutes and Willamette national forest lands comprise the 285,202-acre preserve set aside by Congress as the Three Sisters Wilderness. One of more than 650 units of the National Wilderness Preservation System, it is a majestic piece of the remaining western wilderness that Wallace Stegner once called "the geography of hope."

It wasn't always so. First the idea and then the fact of the "enduring resource of wilderness" eventually promised by the Wilderness Act of 1964 had to evolve with American civilization.

From landfall at Jamestown in 1607, the Euro-Americans who occupied that expanse of North America that became the United States struggled for three centuries to carve a civilization out of the wilderness. During those centuries wilderness was, to them, an adversary to be conquered. A frontier ethic prevailed. Public land laws called for disposal, and private greed answered with trespass and fraud, resource waste, and environmental destruction. Americans were too busy subjugating the land—and its native population, to whom the land was not a wilderness but a home—to think about stewardship of the land, and preservation of the wilderness did not occur to many of them.

But, as civilization advanced and progress reduced wilderness to mere "islands in a tamed continent,"[1] the wisdom of "saving the wilderness remnants in America"[2] began to be recognized. Scarcity of wilderness, it seems, was the precondition of its salvation. Only when it became scarce did wilderness become valued. This scarcity eventually led a number of individuals and organizations toward efforts to preserve what remained.

The American Conservation Movement
and the Wilderness Movement

The wilderness movement that eventually produced the National Wilderness Preservation System grew out of the American conservation movement of the late nineteenth and early twentieth centuries. Earlier still, however, pioneer conservationists had warned that the nation's natural resources were being depleted and degraded at an alarming rate, and offered a variety of solutions. Some even suggested that unspoiled public lands should be protected from exploitation and preserved in their natural state. One of the first to embrace this idea was philosopher Henry David Thoreau. His belief that wilderness was an essential source of American character and strength led him to declare "In wildness is the preservation of the world."[3] But these early conservationists' views and warnings were ignored and even vigorously opposed by the majority who believed—or wanted to believe—that the country's forests, waters, wildlife, and other natural resources would last forever. Suggestions of preserving wilderness were particularly ridiculed. A conceptual chasm between pioneer conservationists and their fellow citizens had to be bridged.

George Perkins Marsh, a brilliant and versatile scholar and statesman from Vermont who traveled widely in the United States and abroad, began to bridge that chasm. As a diplomat in Europe and the Middle East, Marsh saw firsthand how centuries of abuse had degraded the ancient lands of the Mediterranean Basin and destroyed the empires those lands once supported. In 1864, just before the end of the Civil War revived Manifest Destiny's push westward, Marsh warned in his book *Man and Nature* "that a desolation, like that which has overwhelmed many once beautiful and fertile regions of Europe, awaits...the United States...unless prompt measures are taken to check the action of destructive causes already in operation."[4] In this book, Marsh deflated the illusion that the United States' natural resources were inexhaustible, and set forth many basic principles of natural resource conservation that remain valid. Perhaps most important, he actually influenced both the public and the politicians to the extent that he is generally recognized as "the father of American conservation."

Marsh was also an early wilderness proponent. "Man is everywhere a disturbing agent," he wrote. "Wherever he plants his foot, the harmonies of nature are turned to discords."[5] And, perhaps anticipating the wilderness movement, he suggested setting aside reserves of "American soil...as far as possible, in its primitive condition."[6]

Taking their cues from Marsh, many early conservationists focused on protecting forests to assure timber and water supplies essential to economic growth. Others sought parks and preserves for recreational and spiritual benefits or fish and game habitat protection. As early as 1872 President Ulysses S. Grant signed the act of Congress that established Yellowstone National Park "as a public park or pleasuring ground for the benefit and enjoyment of the people" at their behest.

This act, which provided for "the preservation…of all timber, mineral deposits, natural curiosities or wonders" of the new national park "and their retention in their natural condition" also "established for the first time the policy of national ownership of superlative resources for the common good."[7] It also inadvertently preserved some wilderness. This setting aside process, not yet a conscious effort to preserve wilderness, continued with establishment of additional national parks and passage of the **Forest Reserve Act of 1891** authorizing the president to designate parts of the West's vast public domain as forest reserves administered by the Department of the Interior. The **Cascade Range Forest Reserve**, proclaimed by President Grover Cleveland on September 28, 1893, included the future Three Sisters Wilderness.

By the beginning of the twentieth century, the conservation movement was well under way, and at least the seeds of a wilderness movement had been sown. But, as the conservation movement evolved, it became apparent that conservation meant different things to different people. Some conservationists, it turned out, were **preservationists**, and others were **utilitarians**.

John Muir emerged as the movement's leading preservationist. Born in Scotland in 1838, Muir immigrated to Wisconsin with his family at age eleven. A harsh childhood on the farm preceded brief studies at the University of Wisconsin, years of odd jobs in factories, and extensive ramblings during which he trained himself as a naturalist and kept detailed journals of his experiences, observations, and reflections on the human relationship to nature. A year before he arrived in San Francisco in 1868, Muir revealed the **biocentric**—or "nature centered"—philosophy that informed his view of wilderness when he wrote in his journal:

> The world we are told was made for man. A presumption that is totally unsupported by the facts. There is a very numerous class of men who are cast into painful fits of astonishment whenever they find anything, living or dead, in all God's universe, which they cannot eat or render in some way what they call useful to themselves. … Nature's object in making animals and plants might possibly be first of all the happiness of each one of them, not the creation of all for the happiness of one. Why ought man to value himself as more than an infinitely small composing unit of the one great unit of creation, and what creature of all that the Lord has taken the pains to make is less essential to the great completeness of that unit?[8]

Muir soon found his way from San Francisco to the Sierra Nevada where, while working as a sheepherder, he came upon Yosemite Valley and his life's calling. Muir's remaining 45 years—except for the 1880s decade he spent managing his wife's fruit ranch hear Martinez,

California—were spent exploring and writing about wilderness. The best parts of nature, his philosophy held, should be preserved as inviolate sanctuaries for animals and plants themselves as well as for the health of the human spirit. Muir's active efforts to protect the Sierra and other wild places from destructive grazing and logging made him what Stewart Udall termed "a sort of Senator-at-large for the American outdoors"9 and the nation's first leading advocate of wilderness preservation. During the 1890s he inspired the legislation that created Yosemite, Sequoia, and General Grant (added to Kings Canyon National Park established in 1939) national parks. He also founded the Sierra Club to carry on his fight for the wilderness.

Although he emphasized the intrinsic value of wilderness, Muir was politically savvy enough to extol its virtue as a recreational resource in statements such as: "Thousands of tired, nerve-shaken, over-civilized people are beginning to find out that going to the mountains is going home; that wilderness is a necessity; and that mountain parks and reservations are useful not only as fountains of timber and irrigating rivers, but as fountains of life."10

Gifford Pinchot was Muir's opposite. He was born in 1865 into a wealthy and well-connected New York family and, after Yale, studied forestry in Europe to become the first American-born professional forester. Appointed to head the Bureau of Forestry in the Department of Agriculture in 1898, Pinchot was a forester without forests to manage; the forest reserves set aside beginning in 1891 remained under the Department of the Interior. Pinchot was, however, a close friend of Vice President Theodore Roosevelt who, upon President William McKinley's assassination in 1901, became president. During President Roosevelt's first term, Pinchot criticized the Interior Department's administration of the forest reserves as "crooked and incompetent,"11 and pushed his idea that America's forests should not be "locked up" in reserves but both "saved" and "used" through scientific management.

Once Roosevelt was elected in his own right in 1904, Pinchot prevailed upon the President and the Congress to put him in charge of the forest reserves. In 1905, the reserves were transferred to the Department of Agriculture's new Forest Service with Pinchot as Chief Forester. In March 1907, the forest reserves were renamed national forests. Later that year, a group of western senators who opposed Pinchot's policies and the President's forest reserve authority managed repeal of the Forest Reserve Act of 1891. Moving quickly, President Roosevelt huddled with Pinchot to name 21 new national forests totaling 16 million acres before he signed the bill that tied his hands. By then presidents Harrison,

Naturalist John Muir and forester Gifford Pinchot clashed over the meaning of conservation and split the American conservation movement.

Cleveland, and Roosevelt had set aside 132 million acres. And, by the time a dispute with President William Howard Taft caused Pinchot to resign as head of his beloved Forest Service in 1910, the National Forest System had grown to 148 million acres and the land base for wilderness preservation had been established.

Although this National Forest System—later expanded to 191 million acres—included a good part of today's National Wilderness Preservation System, wilderness preservation was not part of Pinchot's program. Pinchot defined conservation, a term he claimed to have coined, as "the wise use of the earth and its resources for the lasting good of man. Conservation," he explained, "is the foresighted utilization, preservation, and/or renewal or forests, waters, lands and minerals for the greatest good of the greatest number for the longest time."[12] If there was room for wilderness—as there seems to have been—in his definition of conservation, Pinchot hasn't been credited with seeing it. Instead, his philosophy is viewed as an **anthropocentric**—or "human-centered"—utilitarian approach in which wilderness preservation is considered a waste of natural resources.

Inevitably, Muir's preservationism and Pinchot's utilitarianism collided. They clashed first over sheep grazing on western public ranges, but foremost over San Francisco's plan to improve the city's water and power supplies by damming the Tuolumne River in Yosemite National Park's beautiful **Hetch Hetchy Valley**. Muir considered this valley "a second Yosemite." After a twelve-year fight, during which the latent philosophical split in the American conservation movement between preservationists and utilitarians was laid bare as never before, Muir lost the battle to preserve Hetch Hetchy. Congress authorized the dam in December 1913, and Muir died in December 1914. But, in a sense, Muir won. His genius for publicity kept the violation of Yosemite National Park from establishing a precedent. It also helped inspire passage of the National Park Act of 1916 which established the National Park Service in the Department of the Interior "to conserve the scenery and the natural and historic objects and the wildlife therein and to provide for the enjoyment of the same in such manner and by such means as will leave them unimpaired for the enjoyment of future generations." The national parks have been kept virtually inviolate ever since.

Muir envisioned the national parks as wilderness preserves. But, when the 1916 act charged the new National Park Service with the contradictory missions of protecting the natural integrity of the parks while making them accessible for use by the public, wilderness was poised to suffer. Stephen T. Mather, an admirer of Muir and the visionary founding director of the Park Service, was interested in the parks as natural preserves, but was forced by practical politics to promote the parks through commercial tourism. Wilderness wouldn't sell the fledgling National Park System, but development for recreation would. Mather emphasized construction of roads, hotels, and other facilities to attract and accommodate visitors. It wasn't long before "the promotional zeal that would become so characteristic of national park administration as a result of the 1916 act curbed the service's role as a pioneer in wilderness management...."[13] The wilderness concept had to develop elsewhere.

Aldo Leopold and Arthur Carhart: U.S. Forest Service Wilderness Pioneers

Ironically, it was Pinchot's utilitarian Forest Service that pioneered federal wilderness preservation and management beginning in the second decade of the twentieth century. The two leading Forest Service wilderness pioneers of this time were forester **Aldo Leopold** and landscape architect **Arthur Carhart**.

As early as 1913, Leopold—then the young, Yale-educated supervisor of the Carson National Forest in New Mexico—had discussed

Aldo Leopold and Arthur Carhart of the U.S. Forest Service pioneered wilderness preservation on the National Forest System.

setting aside wilderness areas in the national forests with Elliott Barker, one of his rangers. His original interest was wilderness recreation. But, by the end of World War I, he saw expansion of roads into national forest backcountry as a threat to a full range of natural and cultural values. Wilderness, Leopold echoed Thoreau, "was the forge on which the American national character had been created, and loss of wilderness regions deprived the country of a source of having this heritage."[14] And, as an early ecologist, he saw in wilderness "an ideal laboratory for the study of natural processes."[15] In a 1919 *Journal of Forestry* article, Leopold proposed a wilderness of at least 500,000 acres for each of the eleven states west of the Great Plains.

Meanwhile, Carhart—the Forest Service's first full-time landscape architect—had come to similar conclusions. In 1919, the young "recreation engineer" in the agency's Denver district office (called "regional offices" since 1930) was assigned to survey a road around Trappers Lake in the White River National Forest of Colorado, and to locate summer home sites on the lakeshore. Carhart came away from the job convinced that the best use of the area would be wilderness recreation. His recommendation against development was a bold move for a junior Forest Service employee, and Carhart was pleasantly surprised when District Forester Carl J. Stahl took the "unprecedented step in Forest

Service history"[16] of designating Trappers Lake an area to be kept road-less and undeveloped. It remains so today as part of the Flat Tops Wilderness.

In December 1919, before that Trappers Lake designation, Leopold, then assistant district forester in Albuquerque, visited Carhart in Denver. "The Forest Service," Carhart observed, " is obligated to make the greatest return from the [National Forest System] to the people...that is possible." But, as he expressed the issue:

There is...a great wealth of recreational facilities and scenic values within the Forests, which have not been so utilized and...the Service is face to face with a question of big policies, big plans, and big utilization for these values and areas.[17]

Then, perhaps to help Leopold address that issue, Carhart wrote in a supplementary "memorandum to Mr. Leopold":

There is a definite point in different types of country where man-made structures should be stopped.[18] There is a limit to the...shorelines on the lakes; there is a limit to the number of lakes...; there is a limit to the mountainous areas of the world; and...there are portions of natural scenic beauty which are God-made, and...which of right should be the property of all people.[19]

Encouraged by Carhart, Leopold pressed on with his plans for larger wilderness preserves. In a 1921 *Journal of Forestry* article, he urged that "representative portions of some forests be preserved as wilderness." And he defined wilderness as "a continuous stretch of country preserved in its natural state, open to lawful hunting and fishing, big enough to absorb a two weeks' pack trip, and kept devoid of roads, artificial trails, cottages, or other works of man."[20] In the same article he acknowledged that preserving wilderness would seem "rank heresy to some minds" but argued that this "highest recreational use" for certain lands could coexist with Pinchot's utilitarian doctrine. And, at the end of the article, he recommended that an undeveloped portion of the Gila National Forest in New Mexico be set aside as a permanent wilderness reserve.

Early in 1922, Southwestern District Forester Frank C.W. Pooler authorized Leopold to inspect and develop a plan for managing the proposed reserve. Leopold's 1922 plan, opposed by some of his district office colleagues who favored development over preservation, was eventually approved by Pooler. The 574,000-acre **Gila Wilderness Reserve**—"America's first wilderness"—was officially designated on June 3, 1924. By the end of 1925, the Forest Service had set aside five more wilderness reserves and "had taken the fundamental step of acknowledging wilderness values."[21]

These values echoed in the Pacific Northwest, where North Pacific District Forester Christopher M. Granger issued wilderness area selection and management instructions to his forest supervisors in January 1926. "Proposed wilderness areas," he emphasized, should be selected carefully...

...since their appearance on the forest plan will mean ... that a definite objective is set up of keeping the area in its present primeval inaccessible condition for the use and enjoyment of people who delight in the preservation of the original wilderness mode of travel and use. Areas already opened by road construction or where the transportation system is planned to pass through for the development of [an area], can not be considered for this classification, neither can areas having much value for timber growing, water storage, or other valuable resources, or areas having sufficient charm and natural beauty to attract intensive recreation use by large numbers of people.[22]

The March 1926 Deschutes National Forest recreation plan suggested "the Three Sisters region [be classified] a Wilderness area, since it is at present susceptible to this use."[23]

Wilderness pioneers Leopold and Carhart led the way, during their Forest Service years, toward federal wilderness preservation and management. Their efforts resulted in "the first allocation of public land specifically for wilderness values in American history, and indeed in the world."[24] In a sense, and within a decade, some of Gifford Pinchot's bureaucratic sons had become some of John Muir's philosophical sons. And others in the Forest Service followed for a variety of reasons. Some agreed that preserving wilderness was the right thing to do. Others followed for a political reason: outdoor recreation in wild country was becoming more popular and gaining a larger constituency. Still others followed for a bureaucratic reason: preserving wilderness on national forest lands was preferable to those lands being transferred from Forest Service to National Park Service control.

Leon F. Kneipp, the L-20 Regulation, and the Three Sisters Primitive Area

One who followed was Chief Forester William B. Greeley who, by 1926, had approved the concept of wilderness preservation and encouraged his district foresters to emulate the Gila example. Also, in that year, he directed Assistant Chief Forester **Leon F. Kneipp**, another Leopold-inspired forester and "little sung hero of the movement"[25] to

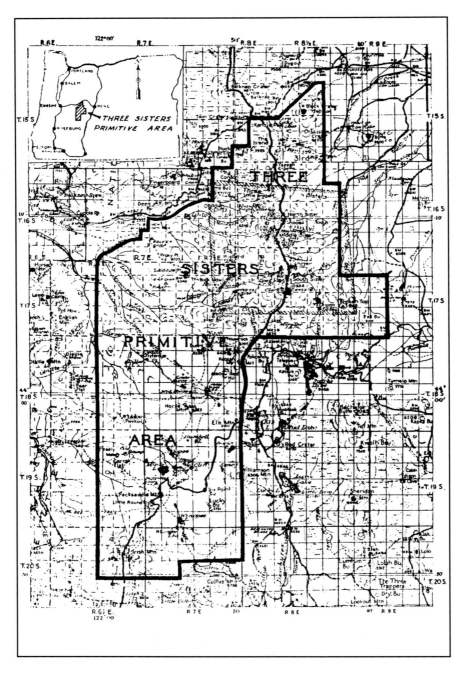

The Three Sisters Primitive Area was designated on the Deschutes and Willamette national forests in 1937.

inventory all undeveloped national forest areas larger than 230,400 acres. Then, in his 1927 annual report, Greeley stated that "the Forest Service believes it to be in the public interest to retain a substantial number of large roadless areas within which some of the most attractive, rugged, and inspiring sections of our mountain country will remain for at least a long time in substantially their natural condition."[26] This report reflected Greeley's belief that wilderness was an important National Forest System resource—even though his view of wilderness emphasized "temporary withdrawals from haphazard development"[27] of resources rather than the "enduring resource of wilderness" called for by Congress thirty years later.

In 1929, when Kneipp's completed inventory reported that 74 roadless tracts totaling 55 million acres remained on national forest lands, the Forest Service issued the **L-20 Regulation** that formalized establishment and protection of **primitive areas**. According to this regulation:

The Chief of the Forest Service shall determine, define, and permanently record…a series of primitive areas…within which will be maintained primitive conditions of environment, transportation, habitation, and subsistence, with a view to conserving the value of such areas for purposes of public education and recreation. Within any area so designated…no occupancy under special use permit shall be allowed, or the construction of permanent improvements by any public agency be permitted, except as authorized by the Chief of the Forest Service or the Secretary [of Agriculture].[28]

By 1933, the Forest Service had established 63 primitive areas totaling over 8.4 million acres. But the magnificent Three Sisters country in the High Cascades of Central Oregon was not among them. Only after certain boosters in Bend had promoted a Three Sisters National Monument under National Park Service administration did the supervisors of the Deschutes and Willamette national forests recommend primitive area designation. Finally, in 1937, eight years after the L-20 Regulation was issued, the **Three Sisters Primitive Area** was designated by Chief Ferdinand A. Silcox. These 191,108 acres of Deschutes and Willamette national forest land included the Three Sisters and Broken Top mountains, several lesser peaks and cinder cones, other volcanic features, alpine meadows, forests, and lakes. In 1938, an additional 55,620 acres that included the French Pete Creek watershed and the Olallie Mountain country were added to the western side of the primitive area.

Although the L-20 Regulation was a "major milestone in the systematic identification and preservation of wilderness,"[29] it amounted to no more than "strong recommendations to Forest Service field personnel suggesting limitations on unplanned development in untouched areas."[30] It didn't actually prohibit development and use. In the North Pacific Region, the limitations of the L-20 Regulation were reflected in a September 1934 memorandum from Assistant Regional Forester F.V. Horton to the region's forest supervisors. "Classification of primitive areas [under the regulation]," he wrote, "is not a legalistic process and causes no change in the legal status of the lands so classified. In essence, it is an administrative act somewhat in the nature of an elaboration of the plan of management for [a national forest]."[31] Thus the agency remained mostly a "timber-cuttin', fire-fightin' outfit" only modestly interested in preservation.[32] Road building, logging, grazing, and other activities continued in most primitive areas. Indeed, most students of early Forest Service wilderness policy agree that the main reason for the L-20 Regulation was not wilderness preservation but turf preservation. By demonstrating the Forest Service's interest in wilderness, more transfers of national forest lands to National Park Service administration might be prevented. Most of the national parks established since passage of the National Park Act of 1916 had been carved out of national forests. Real wilderness preservation on the national forests remained a step or two in the future.

Bob Marshall, the U Regulations, and the Three Sisters Wilderness Area

Bob Marshall took the next major step toward a Forest Service wilderness preservation program. The son of a wealthy New York attorney, Marshall was known for his prowess as a hiker and his passion as a wilderness advocate. Equipped with a master's degree in forestry from Harvard, he worked for the Forest Service in the Rocky Mountains during the 1920s. In 1928, he was one of a score of foresters who discussed wilderness preservation at a meeting in Missoula, where there was little sympathy for the idea, and soon thereafter outlined his views in the agency's newsletter. He then took a leave of absence to earn a doctorate in plant pathology at Johns Hopkins University and travel to Alaska. After a year in the Arctic, Marshall arrived in Washington, D.C., in 1931. There he campaigned for wilderness preservation even as he wrote the recreation section of *A National Plan for American Forestry*—the so-called *Copeland Report*—issued by the U.S. Senate in 1933, and took over the Forestry Division of the U.S. Office of Indian Affairs that same year.

Bob Marshall, as head of the U.S. Forest Service's new Division of Recreation and Lands in the late 1930s, developed the U Regulations that led to reclassification of many primitive areas as wilderness areas and wild areas.

In 1935, Marshall joined Aldo Leopold and a few other wilderness advocates to found the Wilderness Society "for the purpose of fighting off invasion of the wilderness and stimulating…an appreciation of its…emotional, intellectual, and scientific values."[33] Then, in May 1937, Marshall rejoined the Forest Service when Chief Silcox appointed him head of the Washington Office's new Division of Recreation and Lands and encouraged him to strengthen the primitive area system. Marshall made the most of this opportunity, and began a "remarkable crusade to preserve all remaining large roadless areas in the West. Between 1937 and 1939 there was probably no undeveloped area over 100,000 acres on national forest land that he did not recommend to regional foresters to be considered for primitive classification"[34] or inclusion in enlarged primitive areas. Both the setting aside of the Three Sisters Primitive Area in 1937 and the addition of 55,620 acres to its western side in 1938 were direct results of Marshall's efforts. By 1939, when a heart attack felled Marshall at age 38, the Forest Service was managing about 14 million acres as primitive areas.

Also by 1939, in response to concern that the L-20 Regulation was not sufficiently protective of wilderness values, Marshall and his staff had developed the **U Regulations** ("U" being the Forest Service's designation for Marshall's division) to reclassify and strengthen protection of primitive areas. These regulations, which superseded the L-20 Regulation, were signed by Secretary of Agriculture Henry A. Wallace and issued by the Forest Service on September 29, 1939, just two months before Marshall's untimely death.

Under the U Regulations, primitive areas were to be reviewed for reclassification as wilderness areas, wild areas, or roadless areas. **Wilderness areas**, pursuant to Regulation U-1, were "national forest lands in single tracts of not less than 100,000 acres" designated by the Secretary of Agriculture, on recommendation of the Chief of the Forest Service, that "will not be modified or eliminated except by order of the Secretary." **Wild areas**, under Regulation U-2, were "tracts of national forest lands between 5,000 and 100,000 acres that could be established, modified, or eliminated by the Chief of the Forest Service." Wilderness areas and wild areas were managed the same, and management plans were required. Timber cutting, road building, most motorized transportation, and special use permits for such developments as resorts, summer homes, and hunting camps were prohibited. Grazing, water resource development, and mining were allowed to continue under stricter supervision. In short, the U Regulations provided for much more protection of wilderness values than the L-20 Regulation they replaced. A third U Regulation established roadless areas to be managed principally for recreational use "substantially in their natural condition." The only such area ever set aside is now the Boundary Waters Canoe Area Wilderness on the Superior National Forest in Minnesota.

Marshall's death in 1939 followed by World War II's increased demands on the National Forest System for wartime production slowed Forest Service review and reclassification under the U Regulations to a virtual standstill. The process resumed, but only slowly, after the war. Only two million acres had been reclassified by the late 1940s. "The sluggish process troubled wilderness proponents; while the review process stagnated, many areas containing wilderness values were lost..."[35] to other uses. One of these other uses was developed recreation for rapidly growing numbers of outdoor recreationists. Others involved commodity—especially timber—production. As the post-war construction boom increased the demand for national forest timber, Forest Service managers used the U Regulation review and reclassification process to remove commercially valuable timberlands from protected status. The first such attempt, in 1950, proposed removal of about 75,000 acres from the Gila Primitive Area. That effort failed only after the personal intervention of Senator Clinton P. Anderson of New Mexico. But others succeeded, and revealed the defects in the process.

"Perhaps the best-known example of the defects of reclassification took place on the Willamette National Forest in the mid-1950s"[36] when that forest and the Deschutes National Forest reviewed the Three Sisters Primitive Area for reclassification as the Three Sisters Wilderness Area. During this process, the Forest Service proposed in 1954 to modify the primitive area's boundaries by eliminating most of the 55,620 acres added to the western side in 1938 and adding 5,532 acres to the northern and eastern sides. The resulting Three Sisters Wilderness Area would contain 196,640 acres astride the Cascade crest, and would stretch about 32 miles north to south and average about 12 miles east to west.

The most controversial aspect of the Forest Service proposal, which set the western boundary at Horse Creek, was elimination of most of the 1938 western addition on the grounds that those lands "of normal for-ested character" contained "nothing of especially outstanding scenic quality."[37] Assistant Secretary of Agriculture E.L. Peterson agreed that the lands under consideration "were not predominantly valuable for wilderness."[38] This proposal was supported by most timber interests and opposed by wilderness advocates who wanted some or all of the western addition retained. The map on page 16 shows the western boundaries proposed by the Forest Service and others and the northern and eastern additions proposed by the Forest Service.

On February 3, 1957, after several years of spirited controversy and over 17 years after issuance of the U Regulations, the Secretary of Agriculture established the **Three Sisters Wilderness Area** of about 197,000 acres. A close approximation of the Forest Service proposal, this area excluded the disputed low-elevation timberlands west of Horse Creek and included some of the additions proposed for its northern and eastern reaches. As the official U.S. Department of Agriculture press release put it:

The Department decision designated Horse Creek as the western boundary of the Three Sisters Wilderness Area. During the re-study of this area a controversial issue developed around whether the 53,000-acre area west of Horse Creek should be in the [wilderness area] or whether it would have more public value under multiple-use management and for timber production on a sustained-yield basis.

In arriving at a decision the Department pointed out that the importance of wilderness as a resource was fully recognized but that it is necessary to maintain a proper balance between areas set aside for wilderness and those for multiple-purpose use.

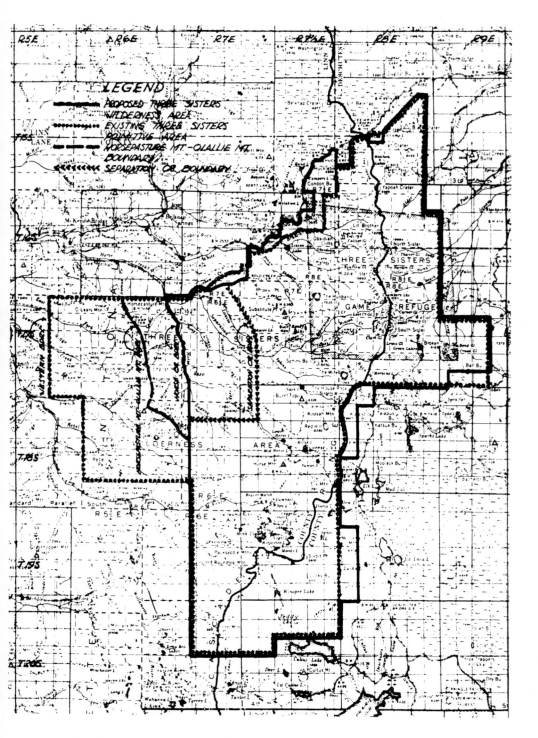

The effort to reclassify the Three Sisters Primitive Area as the Three Sisters Wilderness Area involved a struggle over the area's western boundary.

As for the lands excluded from the new wilderness area, the release continued:

> The decision ordered that a careful multiple-use management plan be prepared for the 53,000 acres west of Horse Creek. In line with the multiple-use policy governing the management of the national forests, the Service was instructed that this plan provide full protection to the adjacent wilderness areas, that sections of special botanical and geographical significance be preserved, and that camping and picnicking facilities for family recreation be established.

Such decisions, reflecting the relatively low priority accorded wilderness, convinced wilderness advocates that additional, more permanent protection was needed. After all, the U Regulations' wilderness areas and wild areas, although protected better than L-20 Regulation primitive areas, remained administrative, not statutory reserves. They could be established or eliminated by the Secretary of Agriculture or the Chief of the Forest Service at the stroke of a pen. They existed at the discretion of cabinet officers and bureaucrats. They lacked the protection of law. Therefore, in the late 1950s and early 1960s, preservationists sought statutory rather than administrative protection of wilderness.

Howard Zahniser, the Wilderness Act of 1964, and the Three Sisters Wilderness

Howard Zahniser, a charter member and, since 1945, the executive director of the Wilderness Society, led the fight for statutory protection of wilderness. In 1956, after playing a key role in the successful defense of Dinosaur National Monument against the Bureau of Reclamation's plan to build Echo Park Dam as part of the Upper Colorado River Storage Project—a major victory that encouraged and united wilderness advocates, Zahniser drafted a wilderness bill. On June 7, 1956, Senator **Hubert H. Humphrey** of Minnesota introduced this eloquently written bill in the U.S. Senate. Four days later, Representative **John P. Saylor** of Pennsylvania introduced a companion bill in the House of Representatives. Eight years of often-heated debate ensued. These years included 18 hearings in Washington, D.C., and the West—including one in Bend, Oregon, in 1958—and 66 revisions of the bill, 20 of which passed either the Senate or the House.

The wilderness bill was consistently supported by most conservation and preservation organizations and consistently opposed by most commodity interests. Senator Richard L. Neuberger of Oregon, who had fought the 1957 decision to reduce the Three Sisters Wilderness

Howard Zahniser, executive director of the Wilderness Society from 1948 until his death in 1964, led the fight to pass the Wilderness Act of 1964 and to establish the National Wilderness Preservation System.

Area, was a co-sponsor of the bill and its "most ardent congressional advocate until his death in 1960."[39] Senator Wayne Morse of Oregon also supported the bill.

At first, the Forest Service opposed the wilderness bill. After all, it already had established administrative wilderness areas, including the Three Sisters Wilderness Area, in many parts of the National Forest System. Although "the management provisions of this bill were essentially the same as Regulation U-1" that governed those wilderness areas, Chief Richard A. McArdle testified in 1957 against an "excessively restrictive bill" that "would strike at the heart of the multiple-use policy of national forest administration."[40] As late as 1961, Supervisor David R. Gibney of the Willamette National Forest told public meetings in Eugene that the wilderness bill "was a scheme to lock up timber resources and prepare the way for conversion of the entire wilderness system into national parks."[41] But the Forest Service's opposition changed to support after Congress passed the Multiple-Use Sustained-Yield Act of 1960 that reaffirmed the agency's multiple-use management authority, and after President John F. Kennedy voiced support for wilderness legislation.

Ultimately, the key to passage was Zahniser's tireless devotion and pragmatic temperament that guided the bill through "a process of drawing together support for the wilderness system and chipping away at the opposition through a series of compromises aimed primarily at commercial users."[42] Grazing and mining interests were the bill's most powerful opponents, and their influence was reflected in concessions to grazing and mining in wilderness. Finally, on April 9, 1963, the Senate passed a weakened wilderness bill by a vote of 73 to 12. By a vote of 373 to one, the other members either absent or abstaining, the House passed it on July 30, 1964. On September 3, 1964, a few months after Zahniser's death at 58, President Lyndon B. Johnson signed the Wilderness Act, and the United States became the first nation in the world to pass a law to protect wilderness.

Passage of the Wilderness Act, Chief Edward P. Cliff claimed in 1965, "made it plain that Congress approved of the areas [the Forest Service had set aside under the U Regulations] as 'wilderness' and 'wild' areas..." and "endorsed in principle the wilderness concepts and management practices the Forest Service had been pioneering for four decades."[43]

The **Wilderness Act of 1964** declared it to be the policy of Congress "to secure for the American people of present and future generations the benefits of an enduring resource of wilderness." To implement this policy, the Act (1) defined wilderness, (2) established the National Wilderness Preservation System, (3) provided management guidance for that system, and (4) provided for growth of that system.

The Wilderness Act defined wilderness, "in contrast with those areas where man and his own works dominate the landscape," as "an area where the earth and its community of life are untrammeled by man, where man himself is a visitor who does not remain." Zahniser had chosen the word *untrammeled* to reflect his view of wilderness as "not subject to human controls and manipulations that hamper the free play of natural forces."[44] Further, according to the Act, congressionally-designated wilderness is specifically defined as "an area of undeveloped federal land retaining its primeval character and influence, without permanent improvements or human habitation, which is protected and managed so as to preserve its natural conditions and which (1) generally appears to have been affected primarily by the forces of nature, with the imprint of man's work substantially unnoticed; (2) has outstanding opportunities for solitude or a primitive and unconfined type of recreation; (3) has at least 5,000 acres of land or is of sufficient size to make practical its preservation and use in an unimpaired condition; and (4) may also contain ecological, geological, or other features of scientific, educational, scenic, or historical value." This definition reflects

Girl Scouts begin a trek into the Three Sisters Wilderness Area in 1960, four years before the Wilderness Act of 1964 designated it the Three Sisters Wilderness.

congressional recognition of the need to balance ideal, untrammeled wilderness with a definition that "accommodates reality by stating that these areas *'generally* appear' to be *'primarily* affected' by nature with man's imprint *'substantially* unnoticeable' [emphasis added]."[45]

In addition to defining wilderness, the Wilderness Act established the **National Wilderness Preservation System** that incorporated the 9.1 million acres of the 54 units on the National Forest System that had been administratively designated as wilderness, wild, or roadless areas under the U Regulations. The **Three Sisters Wilderness** was among these original or "instant" statutory wildernesses. The Act provided management direction for the wilderness system lands that:

> ...shall be administered for the use and enjoyment of the American people in such manner as will leave them unimpaired for future use and enjoyment as wilderness, and so as to provide for the protection of these areas, the preservation of their wilderness character, and for the gathering and dissemination of information regarding their use and enjoyment *as wilderness* [emphasis added].

To ensure that "use and enjoyment" of wilderness didn't adversely affect its integrity "as wilderness," the Act prohibited certain uses and permitted others. Still other permitted uses resulted from compromises necessary to get the Act passed. Prohibited were most commercial enterprises, permanent and temporary roads, motorized transport and mechanized equipment, landing of aircraft, and structures and installations—except for necessary administrative purposes and to protect pre-existing private rights. Special provisions allowed: mining on valid claims and mineral development on leases established by the end of 1983, with mineral prospecting and surveys permitted to provide information on mineral resources; water development projects with presidential approval; livestock grazing; fire, disease, and insect control; and aircraft landings and motorboat use where established. Also allowed were certain commercial uses, such as recreational outfitting and guiding, deemed compatible with the wilderness concept.

Finally, wilderness advocates' conviction that many *de facto* wilderness lands that should be preserved could be preserved by congressional action was reflected in the preamble of the Wilderness Act that was passed "to assure that an increasing population, accompanied by expanding settlement and growing mechanization, does not occupy and modify all areas within the United States…, leaving no lands designated for preservation and protection in their natural condition…." That the Wilderness Act has remained virtually unchanged since passage in 1964 reflects the staying power of its author's vision.

Growth of the National Wilderness Preservation System and the Three Sisters Wilderness

To provide for the growth of the National Wilderness Preservation System, the Wilderness Act of 1964 gave the Forest Service ten years "to study and report on the 'suitability or nonsuitability' for preservation as wilderness of the remaining 5.4 million acres"[46] comprising its residual 34 L-20 Regulation primitive areas. The act also mandated ten-year wilderness studies by the National Park Service and the U.S. Fish and Wildlife Service of all roadless areas larger than 5,000 acres under their management. Passage of the Federal Land Policy and Management Act of 1976 included the Bureau of Land Management and the national resource lands it manages in this process.

During the next decade, the Forest Service completed the primitive area review required by the Wilderness Act, and began its own inventory of other national forest lands that Chief Cliff thought Congress might consider for wilderness designation. This inventory, the first since Kneipp's late 1920s effort, paved the way for the Forest Service's first **Roadless Area Review and Evaluation** (RARE I) effort "to recommend which of the inventoried areas should receive further intensive study for possible wilderness designation."[47] The stringent "purist" approach that the Forest Service adopted for this process—an approach based on a literal reading of the Wilderness Act likely influenced by the agency and its commodity-producing clientele—disqualified from serious consideration many areas that contained "nonconforming features" such as cabins or jeep trails or were influenced by the "sights and sounds of civilization." The results of RARE I shocked preservationists: only 12.3 million acres of about 56 million acres reviewed and evaluated were recommended for wilderness study.

One of the Willamette National Forest roadless areas that didn't make the RARE I cut was the so-called **French Pete** area, a large part of the 1938 western addition to the Three Sisters Primitive Area deleted during the 1957 reclassification as the Three Sisters Wilderness Area. Appeal of Chief John McGuire's 1973 decision that prevented addition of the timber-rich French Pete watershed to the Three Sisters Wilderness, combined with public outrage at other RARE I results, led to passage of the Eastern Wilderness Act of 1975. In this act, Congress directed the Forest Service to relax its wilderness criteria. It led also to RARE II. Although its 1979 "recommendations for wilderness designation of 15.4 million acres were an improvement," RARE II also proved "a major disappointment to preservationists who went to work with individual congressional delegations on a state-by-state basis to formulate and introduce legislation for the creation of designations of a size commensurate with their goals."[48]

In the meantime, politics had removed the French Pete controversy from the RARE I and RARE II arenas. Efforts to "save French Pete" ranged from a 1969 rally at Willamette National Forest headquarters in Eugene to the introduction of legislation by Senator Bob Packwood of Oregon. Many groups and individuals, centered in Eugene and on the University of Oregon campus, fought for French Pete's restoration to the wilderness. Among these, the Save French Pete Committee was the most important. Others included the Friends of the Three Sisters Wilderness, the Oregon Conservation Council, the Eugene Natural History Society, and outdoor clubs like the Obsidians and the Chemeketans. Among individuals, Prince Helfrich, a McKenzie River guide, and Karl Onthank, a former Mazama club official, stood out.[49] Passage of the **Endangered Wilderness Act of 1978**, by a Congress discouraged by RARE I and encouraged by President Jimmy Carter to expand the National Wilderness Preservation System "promptly, before the most deserving federal lands are opened to other uses and lost to wilderness forever,"[50] finally resolved the French Pete controversy by

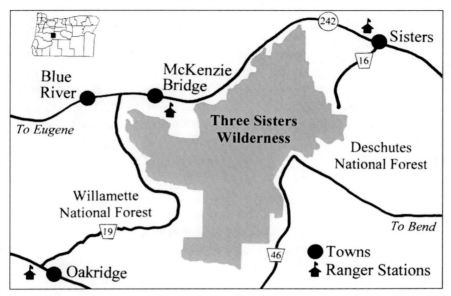

Astride the crest of the Cascade Range, the Three Sisters Wilderness is Oregon's second largest and most visited wilderness.

adding the 45,400-acre area to the Three Sisters Wilderness. This addition was the first fully forested watershed of any size included in the largely "rock and ice" wilderness system. In all, this act set aside 1.3 million acres of new wilderness and wilderness additions in "the largest single addition to the National Wilderness Preservation System since the Wilderness Act of 1964 was passed."[51] These were, for the most part, "areas either excluded from the RARE I inventory of roadless areas or not recommended for wilderness study or classification after their review—thus the name 'endangered wilderness'."[52] This act also reflected Congress' scrutiny of "the Forest Service's 'purity' requirement for wilderness classification, including its 'sights and sounds doctrine',"[53] and confirmed that wilderness could be located near cities and could include areas previously affected by human activity.

The **Oregon Wilderness Act of 1984** added 38,100 acres—much of it by pushing boundaries southward to include the Erma Bell Lakes-Irish Lake-Many Lakes country, northward to include Rainbow Creek and Rainbow Falls, eastward and southward toward the Cascade Lakes Highway, and eastward to include the upper watersheds of Squaw Creek, Park Creek, and Park Meadow—to bring the Three Sisters Wilderness to its current size.

Today, as a result of the Wilderness Act of 1964 and passage of about 120 additional wilderness laws, the "geography of hope" that is the National Wilderness Preservation System adds up to about 670 units—wildernesses—totaling almost 105 million acres. That's about 4.7 percent of the land area of the United States. More than half (56,770,766 acres or about 55 percent) of those wilderness acres lie in Alaska, and most of the rest (41,794,739 acres or about 40 percent) are in the eleven western states. Although the National Park Service administers the most wilderness acreage, most of this is in Alaska; the Forest Service manages the most wilderness in the lower 48 states. About 18 percent of the National Forest System is congressionally-designated wilderness.

The Wilderness Concept, the Wilderness, and the World

The success of the Wilderness Act of 1964 in defining wilderness and the success of that Act and subsequent acts in establishing and enlarging the National Wilderness Preservation System notwithstanding, the wilderness concept remains a "complex cultural construct" that means different things to different people. At one extreme, it is a damnable idea that "locks up" otherwise valuable resources. At the other, it is the romanticizing and perpetuation of pristine nature. Somewhere in the middle, where most people stand, it has long been and generally remains the proposition that preserves wild places for a variety of outdoor recreational and spiritual experiences. And, as Stegner observed, the wilderness is "important to us when we are old simply because it is there—important, that is, simply as an idea."[54]

That idea of wilderness is a function of American culture, a culture in constant change. The concept of wilderness in America, therefore, has evolved and will continue to evolve. During the course of American history, "wilderness has been viewed as a barrier to civilization of the frontier; a romantic and ethereal inspiration to art, literature, and philosophy; a diminishing resource in need of legal protection; and, more currently, a relatively undisturbed landscape that can provide a multitude of biological and social benefits."[55]

The fact that it took eight years of negotiations, 66 versions of the bill, and 18 hearings before Congress passed the Wilderness Act testifies to the difficulty of legally defining and physically embodying this concept. But, in the end, the American people achieved something unique in world history. They established a National Wilderness Preservation System to preserve and protect special places they defined as wilderness. Wilderness, then, has been defined in the law as a special type of place "untrammeled by man, where man himself is a visitor who does not remain."

Yet, "the law," as Frome so eloquently put it, "serves only as a starting point for determining—or discerning—what wilderness really is, what it does, and whom it serves." Wilderness, he continues,

"...is more than a place, but equally an idea, a state of mind, even a dream. While the state of wilderness exists in the mind, it does so only to the degree it exists somewhere on the ground. It becomes worthy of description as wilderness because of any particular purpose it serves. Once it retains that character, however, it serves many purposes."[56]

With this chapter as prologue, it remains to explore the nature and culture of the Three Sisters Wilderness and the administration and stewardship of that particular parcel of Stegner's "geography of hope."

Suggested Readings

Fox, Stephen. *John Muir and His Legacy: The American Conservation Movement.* Boston: Little, Brown and Company, 1981. *The best Muir biography.*

Frome, Michael. *Battle for the Wilderness,* rev. ed. Salt Lake City: The University of Utah Press, 1997.

Leopold, Aldo. *A Sand County Almanac.* New York, Oxford University Press, 1949. *A classic in conservation literature.*

Meine, Curt. *Aldo Leopold: His Life and Work.* Madison: The University of Wisconsin Press, 1988. *The best Leopold biography.*

Nash, Roderick. *Wilderness and the American Mind,* 3rd ed. New Haven and London: Yale University Press, 1982. *The editors of the* Los Angeles Times *listed this book among the one hundred most influential books published in the United States in the last quarter century.*

---

[1] Stegner, Wallace. "A Capsule History of Conservation." *Where the Bluebird Sings to the Lemonade Springs.* (New York: Random House, 1992) 119.

[2] Leopold, Aldo. *A Sand County Almanac.* (New York: Oxford University Press, 1949) 200.

[3] Stegner, 121

[4] Ibid., 123.

[5] Udall, Stewart L. *The Quiet Crisis.* (New York: Holt, Rinehart and Winston, 1963), 77.

[6] Watkins, T.H. "Wilderness and the West." *The West.* Geoffrey C. Ward. (Boston: Little, Brown and Company, 1996) 326.

[7] Everhart, William C. *The National Park Service.* (New York: Praeger Publishers, Inc., 1972) 8.

[8] Fox, Stephen. *John Muir and His Legacy: The American Conservation Movement.* (Boston: Little, Brown and Company, 1981) 52.

[9] Udall, 114.

[10] Nash, Roderick. *Wilderness and the American Mind,* 3rd ed. (New Haven and London: Yale University Press, 1982) 140.

[11] Pinchot, Gifford. *Breaking New Ground.* (New York: Harcourt, Brace, and Co., 1947) 197.

[12] Ibid., 505.

[13] Roth, Dennis. "The National Forests and the Campaign for Wilderness." *Journal of Forest History* (July 1984) 112.

[14] Ibid., 113.

[15] Ibid.

[16] Baldwin, David Nicholas. *The Quiet Revolution: Grass Roots of Today's Wilderness Preservation Movement.* (Boulder, Colorado: Pruett Publishing Company, 1972) 34.

[17] Gallagher, Walter. *The White River National Forest, 1891-1981.* (Glenwood Springs, Colorado: U.S. Department of Agriculture, Forest Service, White River National Forest, 1981) 45.

[18] Frome, Michael. *Battle for the Wilderness,* rev. ed. (Salt Lake City: The University of Utah Press, 1997) 119.

[19] Meine, Curt. *Aldo Leopold: His Life and Work.* (Madison: The University of Wisconsin Press, 1988) 178.

[20] Ibid., 196.

[21] Edwards, Mike. "A Short Hike with Bob Marshall." *National Geographic* (May 1985) 675.

[22] U.S. Department of Agriculture, Forest Service. "Forest Recreation Plan." (Portland, Oregon: North Pacific District, January 26, 1926) 2.

[23] U.S. Department of Agriculture, Forest Service. "Recreation Plan, Deschutes National Forest." (Bend, Oregon: Deschutes National Forest, March 31, 1926) 7.

[24] Nash (1982), 78.

[25] Edwards, 682.

[26] Wilkinson, Charles F., and H. Michael Anderson. *Land and Resource Planning in the National Forests.* (Washington, D.C.: Island Press, 1987) 337.

[27] Ibid., 338.

[28] Ibid.

[29] Nash (1982), 7.

[30] Roth, 115.

[31] Horton, F.V. "Memorandum to Forest Supervisors." (Portland, Oregon: U.S. Department of Agriculture, Forest Service, North Pacific Region, September 28, 1934).

[32] Edwards, 678.

[33] Nash (1982), 7.

[34] Wilkinson, 340.

[35] Stankey, George, and Stephen F. McCool. "Evolving Concepts of Wilderness: Implications for the Management of Fire." *Symposium on Fire in Wilderness and Park Management, March 30-April 1, 1993.* Brown, James K., et. al. (Ogden, Utah: U.S. Department of Agriculture, Forest Service, Intermountain Research Station, 1993).

[36] Roth, 117.

[37] Stone, J. Herbert. "Public Notice: Establishment of Three Sisters Wilderness Area and Mt. Washington and Diamond Peak Wild Areas." (Portland, Oregon: U.S. Department of Agriculture, Forest Service, Pacific Northwest Region, May 28, 1954).

[38] Wilkinson, 343.

[39] Roth, 117.

[40] Wilkinson, 344.

[41] Rakestraw, Lawrence, and Mary Rakestraw. *History of the Willamette National Forest.* (Eugene, Oregon: U.S. Department of Agriculture, Forest Service, Willamette National Forest, 1991) 113.

[42] Roth, 122.

[43] Wilkinson, 345.

[44] Hendee, John C., George H. Stankey, and Robert C. Lucas. *Wilderness Management.* 2nd ed. (Golden, Colorado: North American Press, 1990) 108.

[45] Ibid.

[46] Wilkinson, 345.

[47] Hendee, 130.

[48] Nash, Roderick. "Path to Preservation." *Wilderness* (Summer 1984), 11.

[49] Rakestraw and Rakestraw, 114.

[50] Frome, xxiii.

[51] Zinser, Charles I. *Outdoor Recreation: United States National Parks, Forests, and Public Lands.* (New York: John Wiley & Sons, Inc., 1995) 631.

[52] Browning, James A., John C. Hendee, and Joe W. Roggenbuck. *103 Wilderness Laws: Milestones and Management Direction in Wilderness Legislation, 1964-1987.* (Moscow: University of Idaho, 1988) 5.

[53] Ibid.

[54] Stegner, Wallace. "Wilderness Letter." *Marking the Sparrow's Fall.* Stegner, Page, ed. (New York, Henry Holt and Company, 1998) 112.

[55] U.S. Department of Agriculture, Forest Service, and U.S. Department of the Interior, Bureau of Land Management, National Park Service, and Fish and Wildlife Service. *Wilderness Planning.* (Ninemile Ranger Station, Huson, Montana: Arthur Carhart National Wilderness Training Center, 1995) 1-3.

[56] Frome, 11.

South Sister reflected in Camp Lake, Three Sisters Wilderness.

Chapter Two

KNOWING THE THREE SISTERS WILDERNESS

John Muir once wrote of "a country of wonderful contrasts" in which he saw "frost and fire working together in the making of beauty."[1] He wrote of the High Sierra, but his words apply equally to the High Cascades and especially to the Three Sisters Wilderness.

A grasp of the natural and cultural history of this country of wonderful contrasts that the Wilderness Act of 1964 included in the National Wilderness Preservation System illuminates the "why" and informs the "how" of its preservation as wilderness.

Natural History

The "fire" Muir referred to is **volcanism**, the upwelling of molten rock that produces various landscape features including the volcanoes called the Three Sisters and all other Cascade Range volcanoes. This volcanism results from two related phenomena. The first, **plate tectonics**, is the constant movement of about a dozen large rock slabs or "plates"—each about 50 miles thick—that make up the Earth's rigid outer shell, or crust, and is responsible for most of its geologic change and landforms. The second, **subduction**, is the process by which a sea floor plate is pulled or dragged beneath the margin of a continental plate. Along the west coast of North America, a part of the Pacific Ocean sea floor called the **Juan de Fuca Plate** is subducting beneath that part of the **North American Plate** that includes Oregon. As the sea floor plate sinks beneath the continental plate, strong earthquakes and large volcanoes result. The earthquakes produce fissures and faults through which the superheated and less dense sea floor rocks form magma chambers that rise under tremendous pressure and erupt as volcanoes. This process set the stage for the evolution of the Three Sisters country landscape.

The "frost" Muir referred to is **glaciation**, the erosion and deposition of rock material by a large body of ice—a glacier—advancing slowly down a slope or valley because of its weight and gravity. During the Pleistocene epoch—or Ice Age, the cause of which is still debated by scientists—glaciers advanced and retreated several times in the Cascade Range as the Earth's atmosphere alternately cooled and warmed. As they advanced, these dense rivers of ice cut deeply into the mountains and plateaus, leaving hollowed-out volcanoes, rounded-out

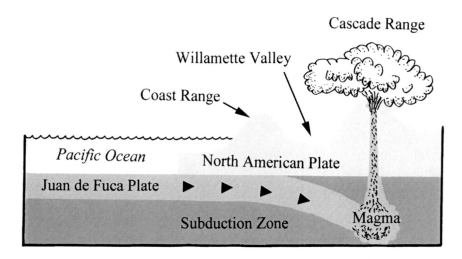

Subduction produces the superheated liquid rock called magma that erupts as volcanoes.

river canyons, and other features when they retreated. This process played a major role in the evolution of the Three Sisters country landscape.

During the 45 million years the Cascade Range in Oregon has been erupting, it has differentiated into two parallel north-south trending ranges—the old **Western Cascades** and the young **High Cascades** in the east. At the same time, the crest of the Cascade Range has migrated eastward from the eastern edge of the Willamette Valley to the current crest of the High Cascades. Most of the country within the Three Sisters Wilderness straddles that crest, and the high, snow-capped Three Sisters and Broken Top at its heart are less than 200,000 years old. However, the western reaches of the wilderness—the country west of Horse Creek and its tributaries that is drained also by Walker, French Pete, and Rebel creeks—belongs to the old Western Cascades. The current landscape of the two parallel ranges evolved simultaneously, and the glaciers emanating from the high country of the younger influenced the evolution of the older.

The evolution of the current High Cascades landscape, and the young volcanic peaks that dominate and lend their name to the Three Sisters Wilderness, began about four and one-half million years ago, late in the Pliocene epoch, when hundreds of major earthquakes

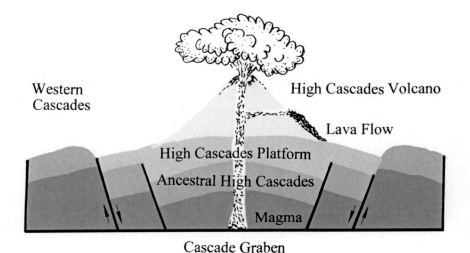

Western Cascades

High Cascades Volcano

Lava Flow

High Cascades Platform

Ancestral High Cascades

Magma

Cascade Graben

Magma erupted through zones of weakness to form the High Cascades Platform and the young High Cascades volcanoes that surmount the platform.

signaled the end of the previous High Cascades range. This ancient range, with its crest at about the same place as the current High Cascades crest, had been built over millions of years by thousands of volcanic eruptions. But, with those earthquakes, the crest of the ancestral High Cascades began to break up and sink within the bounds of roughly parallel north-south trending faults into a great trough called the **Cascade Graben**. While the ancient High Cascades sank, volcanoes erupted within the deepening graben and filled it with lava flows and overlapping shield volcanoes that formed the broad **High Cascades Platform** under which the older mountains were completely buried.

During the latter part of the Ice Age, magma erupted to produce the High Cascades volcanic peaks—including the Three Sisters and Broken Top—that surmount this platform. As these mountains erupted, glaciers advanced and retreated several times. With each advance, the glaciers gouged deeply into the High Cascades and left hollowed-out volcanoes flanked by impressive glacial valleys. The older new High Cascades volcanoes, including North Sister and Broken Top that began to erupt less than 200,000 years ago, were glaciated more than the younger ones, such as South Sister that began to erupt only about 100,000 years ago and continued to erupt until less than two thousand years ago. Glaciers also scoured lake basins in the lower reaches of the High Cascades crest and advanced down the western slope of the platform and into the Western Cascades to broaden stream valleys into characteristic U-shaped glacial canyons. The most recent major advance of the glaciers reached its maximum about 22,000 years ago when ice thickened to perhaps two thousand feet along the High Cascades crest and glaciers reached to within seven miles of where the city of Bend is located. Smaller buttes and cones erupted on and around the Three Sisters and Broken Top during and after the Ice Age, and lava flows from these as well as the larger volcanoes sometimes dammed streams to form lakes and produce other landscape features.

About the same time the ancestral High Cascades began to sink into the Cascade Graben, the old volcanic materials west of the fault were raised about 1,300 feet to an elevation of about 5,000 feet or more and perhaps tilted westward. This increase in elevation and stream gradients resulted in the deep dissection of the valleys of the McKenzie River and its tributaries and the increased relief and drainage patterns of the western reaches of the Three Sisters Wilderness. Subsequent glaciations, the last two of which advanced from the new High Cascades, scoured and lengthened these valleys, especially those of White Branch and Separation creeks that now flow across the western High Cascades Platform east of the fault zone.

The interaction of these complex processes, which continue to shape the Three Sisters Wilderness landscape, erected a mountain barrier that determines the area's weather and climate. This barrier accounts for the wetter west side and dryer east side of the Cascade Range as well as for the more plentiful precipitation and lower temperatures at higher elevations in the mountains.

Precipitation in the Three Sisters country is a result of warm, moist air flowing eastward from the Pacific Ocean, cooling as it rises up the western slope of the Cascade Range, and releasing its moisture as rain or snow. The heaviest precipitation, between 80 and 125 inches annually at the higher elevations, falls on the western side of the High Cascades crest. As the air, drained of much of its moisture, flows eastward over the mountains, descends, and warms, it retains much of its remaining moisture. Lighter precipitation, from about 80 to 40 inches annually within the wilderness and only 12 inches annually in Bend, falls from the crest eastward.

Most precipitation in the Three Sisters country occurs as snowfall between October and June as Pacific Ocean storm systems generated

Moist air from the Pacific Ocean banks against the Three Sisters—and the rest of the Cascade Range—which act as a barrier and account for the wetter west side and dryer east side of the range.

by the **Aleutian Low** bring rain to the Pacific Northwest and abundant snow to the high country. Accumulations reach depths of 20 feet at higher elevations, and snow 10 to 12 feet deep remains on some upper slopes through July. Precipitation is light during the summer months when the **Pacific High** replaces the Aleutian Low, and generally falls as rain during occasional summer thunderstorms. Summer snow-storms are not unusual.

Temperature extremes in the Three Sisters country vary from 80° F. to 90° F. in the summer to -20° F. to -30° F. in the winter. Rapid changes in weather are not unusual

The great range in elevation within the Three Sisters Wilderness—from about 1,850 feet above sea level in the lower French Pete Creek area to the 10,358-foot peak of South Sister—and the consequent great ranges in environmental conditions—aspect, exposure, temperature, precipitation, etc.—result in three distinct regions that provide context for the study of the wilderness's natural history. These are the Alpine Crest Region, the Lower Crest Region, and the Western Plateaus and Canyons Region shown on the map on page 34. A **region** is an area that possesses significant aspects of sameness throughout its extent that differentiate it from adjoining areas. Each of these regions is

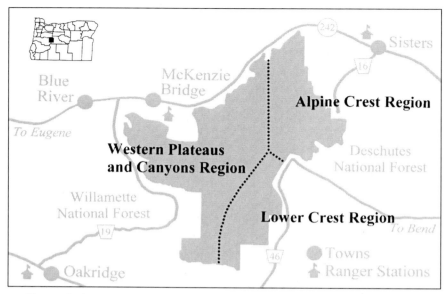

Three distinct regions provide context for understanding Three Sisters Wilderness natural history.

identified by significant common characteristics dominant within it but not dominant within the other two. These distinctive and differentiating characteristics usually are more obvious at the core of each region than along its margins. The boundaries between these regions usually are zones of transition within which one region blends into another, not sharp lines such as the legal boundaries between the Three Sisters Wilderness and the other Deschutes and Willamette national forest lands. The size and diversity expressed in these regions make the Three Sisters Wilderness a refuge for diverse wildlife populations and a home for more plant species than any other Oregon wilderness.

The Alpine Crest Region. The northeastern third of the Three Sisters Wilderness, the environs of the Three Sisters and Broken Top, is a land of high relief and high elevations that range from about 5,200 feet to 10,358 feet above sea level. In addition to the wilderness's major peaks and only glaciers, this complex Alpine Crest Region harbors its best known and most visited lakes, lush wildflower meadows that alternate with arid pumice plains and stark lava flows, and forested slopes that yield to rock and ice at timberline. This region's open alpine beauty, at once rugged and fragile, makes it the most visited and heaviest impacted in the wilderness.

Topography. In 1944, Howel Williams, a University of California geology professor who dispelled what he called "The Myth of Mount Multnomah" (see page 36) as he described the volcanic origin of the Alpine Crest Region in *Volcanoes of the Three Sisters Region*, wrote of its unique topography:

For magnificence of glacial scenery, for wealth of recent lavas, and for graphic examples of dissected volcanoes no part of [the High Cascades] surpasses the area embracing the Sisters.... Seventeen glaciers still survive on the higher peaks; moraine-dammed lakes and ice-cut tarns occur in profusion around their feet; barren sheets of basalt, no more than a few centuries old, cover [large areas]; youthful cinder cones and fresh fields of blocky obsidian add variety to the landscape; and the older volcanoes are so deeply denuded that their central conduits and radial dikes are magnificently displayed.[2]

"During the past few thousand years," Williams wrote, "there has probably been more volcanic activity in the vicinity of the Three Sisters than in any other part of the High Cascades."[3]

The four major peaks of the Alpine Crest Region, the Three Sisters and Broken Top, erupted late in the Ice Age. The now-quiet Three Sisters volcanoes, all over 10,000 feet in elevation and home to more than a dozen glaciers, dominate not just the region but the entire wilderness that bears their name. Each erupted for periods of about 10,000 to 100,000 years, and one will erupt again. Along with nearby extinct Broken Top volcano, these peaks exemplify the changes glaciers can bring to once-symmetrical composite volcanoes.

North Sister, which began to erupt about 150,000 years ago and erupted for about 10,000 years, is the oldest, most glaciated, and most rugged of the Three Sisters. At one time the largest of all at over 11,000 feet, its original surface and from a quarter to a third of its original volume have been glaciated away. Its remaining fragmented summit reaches 10,094 feet, and Lynn, Villard, and Thayer glaciers still cling to its eastern flanks. **Little Brother** (7,810 feet) is a small parasitic cone on North Sister's northwestern side. "While it was enveloped by ice," Williams concluded, "a large cirque was gouged into its western side and its eastern part was almost demolished."[4]

Middle Sister erupted between 150,000 and 50,000 years ago. At 10,053 feet the smallest of the three, Middle Sister retains the most impressive complement of glaciers. Collier Glacier, on the mountain's northern shoulder, is Oregon's second largest. While its western side has been modified only slightly by glaciation, its eastern side has been profoundly changed by erosion of the great amphitheater that hosts the Hayden and Diller glaciers.

THE MYTH OF MOUNT MULTNOMAH

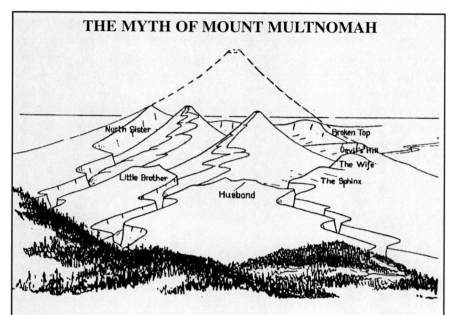

Hodge published this "sketch of the Three Sisters at the present time, showing the rather perfect caldera rim, preserved in the North Sister, Little Brother, the Husband, the Sphinx, the Wife, Devils Hill, and inclosing Middle and South Sisters" to support his Mount Multnomah theory.

A theory advanced in 1925 by University of Oregon geology professor Edwin T. Hodge explained the Three Sisters, Broken Top, and surrounding peaks as remnants of an exploded super-volcano that he called Mount Multnomah.

In 1944, however, University of California geology professor Howell Williams, the United States' leading volcanologist, exploded what he called "the myth of Mount Multnomah." His studies of the Three Sisters region determined each of these peaks to be individual volcanoes and concluded that "Mount Multnomah never existed."

Their works make fascinating reading.

Hodge, Edwin T. *Mount Multnomah: Ancient Ancestor of the Three Sisters.* Eugene: University of Oregon, 1925.

Williams, Howel. *Volcanoes of the Three Sisters Region, Oregon Cascades.* Berkeley: University of California Press, 1944.

South Sister, the youngest and least glaciated of the three, is also the largest and, at 10,358 feet, is Oregon's third highest peak (Mt. Hood is highest and Mt. Jefferson is second highest). Bishop emphasized that South Sister "is not a simple cone [but] a jumble of domes, andesite flows, feeder dikes, and cinder cones that looks like it was assembled by a committee. Glaciers have quarried away the older, softer rocks, with the exception of the dual summit cinder cones [that] erupted after glaciers ceased to be a serious threat 8,000 or 9,000 years ago."[5] As a result, it is the only one of the Three Sisters which still has a summit crater. A corner of this broad crater is occupied by Oregon's highest lake.

Unlike her two northern sisters, which are not likely to erupt again, South Sister, which began to erupt only 100,000 years ago, is alive and well and will erupt again. Eruptions as recent as about 2,000 years ago account for the Rock Mesa flow on its southwestern flank, the Devils Hill chain of lava domes on its southern flank, the Newberry Lava Flow that dammed Fall Creek to impound the Green Lakes, and the adjacent Miller Lava Flow. South Sister's next eruption may occur on its western slope where, in 2000, the U.S. Geological Survey detected a pattern of ground uplift known as "the bulge" which is about 12 miles in diameter and growing in height at a rate of about one inch per year. This bulge is evidence of volcanic material, which could include magma, collecting in pools about 3.5 miles below the surface. Earthquake swarms would precede any eruption of this material. South Sister's many glaciers include Prouty Glacier, on its northeastern slope and Oregon's largest, Lewis and Clark glaciers on the south, and others that radiate like spokes from the summit.

Broken Top, just east of South Sister, is a contemporary of North Sister but had a longer eruptive history. Repeated glaciation during and after this eruptive period, which has eroded away the mountain's former summit—it stood much higher than the jagged summit's current 9,175 feet—as well as its entire southwestern slope and much of its interior, has exposed the core of this composite volcano. As a result, "its internal structure is perfectly displayed" in colorful "bands of red, purple, and black scoria [that] alternate with yellow, brown, and orange lapilli tuffs."[6] The remnant Bend and Crook glaciers survive on its eastern flanks above an unnamed neo-glacial moraine-dam lake. **Cayuse Crater** (7,354 feet) is a conspicuous red cinder cone that erupted on Broken Top's southern slope between 6,000 and 10,000 years ago. After the cone was built, its southern wall was breached by lava flows that split into two branches. One emptied into the canyon of Fall Creek to produce a series of waterfalls; the other poured into the valley of Soda Creek to deflect its course.

A complex of other topographic features surrounds these four major peaks. These include old, small, glaciated volcanoes, relatively new volcanic cones, domes, and flows, a major escarpment, pumice plains, and a major lake basin.

Black Crater (7,251 feet) guards the northern tip of the Three Sisters Wilderness. Because it lies at a lower elevation and its eruptions continued to a later time, Black Crater has suffered less from, but not escaped, glaciation. Its two craters, an eastern one for little Black Crater Lake on the wilderness boundary and "a second, higher chasm that left the peak's summit teetering atop a 500-foot cliff"[7] on the northern slope, were scooped by glaciers, not volcanic features.

A complex array of young volcanoes, cinder cones, and their lava flows and cinder fields dominates the rest of the Alpine Crest Region's northern reaches. Erupting into the last millennium, **Collier Cone** (7,534 feet), **Yapoah Crater** (6,737 feet), and a row of four adjoining cinder cones called **Four-in-One Cone** (6,258 feet) are responsible for the northward lava flows that "poured into the valleys and eddied round the ridges, leaving them as green islands enveloped by black lava."[8] **Huckleberry Mountain** (5,827 feet) is one of these *kipukas*, and **The Island** to the northeast is the largest. Collier and Four-in-One cones joined forces to produce the **Jerry Flow** down the canyon of White Branch Creek that dammed Obsidian and Linton creeks to impound Linton Lake, and volcanic ejecta blown by the wind from Collier Cone covers the **Ahalapam Cinder Field** to the northeast. Collier Cone blocked advances of Collier Glacier, once Oregon's largest, as recently as the 1920s; however, the glacier has melted back more than a mile since then. Unlike many of its neighbors, **Condon Butte** (5,901 feet) didn't emit much lava and retains its symmetry.

South Sister's southern slopes overlook an array of volcanic features that rivals those north of North Sister for beauty and interest. **Rock Mesa** (6,700 feet), the region's most extensive mass of obsidian, erupted on South Sister's southwestern slope about 2,000 years ago to cover about one and one-half square miles before it ended in high banks of blocky talus. "Part of the flow was suddenly chilled to black glass; the rest...frothed into gray pumice."[9] Below is the **Wickiup Plain**, the largest sparsely vegetated plain in the Three Sisters Wilderness. Blanketed by Rock Mesa pumice, this plain owes its undulating appearance to copious volcanic flows. Emanating from many sources, some of these erupted between 10,000 and 20,000 years ago while others are much more recent. **Le Conte Crater** (6,574 feet),

South Sister, Rock Mesa, Le Conte Crater, and the Wickiup Plain, Three Sisters Wilderness.

Tam McArthur Rim and the Tumalo Highlands surmounted by Ball Butte (left) and Broken Top (right), in the Three Sisters Wilderness, rise above Three Creek Lake, just outside the wilderness boundary.

a perfectly preserved cinder cone that erupted since the Ice Age, rises about 200 feet above the Wickiup Plain at the edge of Rock Mesa. Its bowl-shaped crater, about 100 feet deep, sometimes contains a small, early-summer lake filled by melting snow. A ridge projecting southward from the cone's base is a flow that poured from a fissure in its side. Another flow poured northward into the valley of Mesa Creek where large springs discharge from its snout. Le Conte Crater, too, is covered by Rock Mesa pumice. To the east, eruption of **Devils Hill** (about 7,050 feet) and its chain of lava domes, some 2,000 years old, also scattered pumice over the landscape.

Except for the eastern extension of the Three Sisters Wilderness into the **Tumalo Highlands**, built by immense eruptions of pumice and ash during the past half-million years, the eastern margins of the Alpine Crest Region are relatively unremarkable forested drainages. East of Broken Top, glaciers have carved into the northern edge of the highlands at **Tam McArthur Rim** to expose layers of lava flows and ash in a dramatic 500-foot cliff. Just to the south, and about a mile and one-half east of Broken Top's summit, the highlands are surmounted by **Broken Hand** (8,376 feet) and **Ball Butte** (8,091 feet).

The western slopes of the Three Sisters abruptly abut the higher country of the Western Plateaus and Canyons Region of the wilderness.

Hydrography. The prodigious precipitation incident on the Alpine Crest Region—which, in colder times, found expression in the now receding glaciers—collects in snowpacks that melt to maintain the magnificent mountain lakes and streams for which the Three Sisters Wilderness is famous. Still more of this snowmelt percolates through permeable and porous volcanic and glacial soils and rocks to charge not only those spring-fed lakes and streams but also major watersheds of the Deschutes, McKenzie, and Willamette river systems outside the wilderness.

More than a dozen named glaciers, mere remnants of the vast ice caps that buried the High Cascades during Ice Age advances, cluster on the higher slopes of the Three Sisters and Broken Top. Although, as a result of global warming, northern hemisphere glaciers have been shrinking for most of the last century, this remains "the most substantial collection of glaciers in the U.S. outside of Alaska."[10]

Collier Glacier, once Oregon's largest, reflects that trend. When measured in 1925, "it was the largest in the Three Sisters Wilderness: 442 acres of ice starting at the 9,200-foot-high saddle between [North Sister and Middle Sister] and reaching 2.1 miles down to Collier Cone.... But now the glacier's ice covers less than 200 acres and its snout has retreated more than a mile up the mountainside from Collier Cone."[11] While all the glaciers in the Three Sisters country have been shrinking, **Prouty Glacier** on the northeastern slope of South Sister has been melting more slowly than the others and is now Oregon's largest.

Relatively small **Thayer Glacier** and **Villard Glacier** still occupy niches on North Sister. In addition to Collier Glacier, Middle Sister sports **Renfrew Glacier** on its western slope and **Hayden Glacier** and **Diller Glacier** on its eastern slope. And, in addition to the state's largest glacier, South Sister's peak is ringed by the **Carver**, **Lewis** and **Clark**, **Lost Creek**, **Eugene**, and **Skinner** glaciers. Broken Top's eastern face harbors **Bend Glacier** and the smaller **Crook Glacier**. Although heavy snowpacks help insulate these glaciers, they begin to melt later in summers when their insulating snow melts. Streams and lakes turned milky by glacial flour in meltwater evidence this process.

Oregon's highest lake, **Teardrop Pool**, occupies a corner of South Sister's summit crater.

The three **Green Lakes**, nestled between South Sister and Broken Top at just over 6,500 feet above sea level, occupy a glacial basin dammed by a lava flow. About 2,000 years ago, the **Newberry Lava Flow** breached South Sister's southeastern flank and dammed the snowmelt-fed stream that drained the canyon to impound a large lake. Time passed, and that creek—**Fall Creek**—cut a channel around the

The Recession of Collier Glacier

Collier Glacier, between North Sister and Middle Sister and once Oregon's largest, reached Collier Cone in 1927 (top), but had receded more than a mile by 1966 (bottom). As a result of global warming, Northern Hemisphere glaciers have been melting for most of the last century, and Collier Glacier is less than half its size 70 years ago.

The three Green Lakes, which occupy a glacial basin between South Sister and Broken Top, were formed when the Newberry Lava Flow dammed Fall Creek.

eastern end of the blocky obsidian flow. As the creek partially drained the lake and sediments washed into the basin from the surrounding slopes, the original large lake was split into three: **Middle Green Lake** (85 acres, 55 feet deep), **North Green Lake** (7 acres, 20 feet deep), and **South Green Lake** (3 acres, 26 feet deep). Named for its many waterfalls and cascades, Fall Creek begins in a spring just north of North Green Lake, flows into Middle Green Lake at its northeastern end and out at its southwestern end, and tumbles about 1,100 feet in five spectacular miles before it enters Sparks Lake, just south of the wilderness boundary.

    Moraine Lake (12 acres, 23 feet deep), south of South Sister, occupies the U-shaped valley carved by the Lewis Glacier, and is impounded by the rock and sand pushed by the glacier and deposited at its toe as a **moraine**—the rounded ridge that cups the lake on the south and from which the lake takes its name. Later volcanic eruptions scattered pumice across the valley and onto the moraine. Moraine Lake is intermittently drained by **Goose Creek**, extensively fed by springs, into Sparks Lake.

    A number of the region's other lakes, on the higher flanks of the Three Sisters and Broken Top, are neo-glacial **moraine-dam lakes** that came into existence during the twentieth century as the **Little Ice**

Broken Top, a glaciated volcano; the Miller Lava Flow, on South Sister's southeastern slope; and Moraine Lake, impounded by a Lewis Glacier moraine, Three Sisters Wilderness.

Age glaciers melted back. As these glaciers advanced down these mountains—and other High Cascades peaks—they pushed up sand and rock moraines. When the warming trend that ended the 200-year cooler period caused these glaciers to melt and recede up the mountains, water filled the basins behind these loose and erodible moraines during the 1920s and 1930s. As a result, the Three Sisters Wilderness contains more moraine-dam lakes than any other place in the contiguous United States.

Perhaps the oldest of these new lakes is the unnamed lake that formed in the early 1920s at the foot of the Crook Glacier on Broken Top's eastern flank. An October 7, 1966, flash flood that swept down Crater Creek and Soda Creek to cross and close the Cascade Lakes Highway and spill into Sparks Lake, at first blamed on a cloudburst, was really caused by a sudden avalanche of glacial ice that fell into the lake. This avalanche created a wave that overtopped and eroded the lake's moraine dam. The loss of some fifty million gallons of water caused the lake's level to drop 14½ feet and its surface area to decrease from 11 to nine acres. The V-shaped cut eroded in the moraine remains visible. An effort to name Broken Top's lake for Central Oregon writer and historian Phil Brogan has not succeeded.

The failure of the Broken Top lake's moraine dam eventually led to concern about potential hazards associated with other moraine dam

Twentieth Century Moraine-Dam Lakes

Neo-glacial moraine-dam lakes, such as the unnamed lake on Broken Top's eastern flank (top) and Carver Lake on South Sister's northeastern flank (below), came into existence during the twentieth century as glaciers that advanced during the Little Ice Age receded and deposited the moraines that impound the lakes.

South Matthieu Lake and North Sister, Three Sisters Wilderness.

lakes in the region that, in 1986, focused on **Carver Lake** (15 acres, 100 feet deep) on the northeastern flank of South Sister. U.S. Geological Survey scientists found that the lake could breach the unstable natural dam which impounds the lake and create a large mud-flow as flood waters sped down **Squaw Creek**. If the lake drained suddenly, the scientists concluded, the resulting flood would pick up rocks, soil, trees, and debris along its path that would cause the flood to increase in size by as much as two times. This could pose a threat to wilderness visitors immediately downstream from the lake and, about two hours after the moraine dam failure, the muddy flood waters might reach the town of Sisters. Although the scientists could not accurately predict when such a flood might occur, they estimated the risk of occurrence at one to five percent each year. In addition to that on Broken Top, at least two other natural lakes in the Three Sisters Wilderness—**Collier Lake** in the early 1940s and **Diller Lake** in 1970—have breached their moraine dams in the last 60 years. All these events occurred in the late summer or early fall. Carver Lake is the largest and potentially the most hazardous of all these lakes.

Other twentieth century moraine-dam lakes in the region are, from north to south, **Thayer Lake** at the foot of Thayer Glacier on North Sister's eastern flank, mostly-drained Diller Lake at the foot of Diller Glacier on Middle Sister's eastern flank—both drained by tributaries of Squaw Creek, and four of the green **Chambers Lakes** that dot the barren glacial landscape between Middle Sister and South Sister. Northeast of and below these four is **Camp Lake**, not a neo-glacial moraine-dam lake and the only one of the five Chambers Lakes drained by a surface stream, a Squaw Creek tributary.

In the northern reaches of the region, **Yapoah Lake** (10 acres, 25 feet deep) and the diminutive but beautiful **North Matthieu Lake** and **South Matthieu Lake** grace an otherwise lakeless landscape.

In addition to Squaw Creek and its tributaries that drain the Alpine Crest Region toward the northeast, and the previously-described Soda Creek, Fall Creek, and Goose Creek systems that drain the region toward the south, tributaries of Tumalo Creek drain the region toward the east. Several significant tributaries of the McKenzie River rise on the Three Sisters' western slopes to flow into and through the Western Plateaus and Canyons Region.

Flora and Fauna. The plant and animal life of the Alpine Crest Region is as diverse as its landscape. Only a few creeping woody plants, hardy perennials, and lichens and mosses grow at its higher elevations near the peaks of the Three Sisters and Broken Top. But these

Whitebark pine, lodgepole pine, and mountain hemlock near timberline, Three Sisters Wilderness.

rocky heights aren't without notable vegetation. The very small, very rare pumice grapefern, for example, grows on the eastern side of Broken Top above Tam McArthur Rim. Wildlife is limited to the occasional small mammal that ventures this high, "often to meet a tragic end."[12] Though other birds are seen at times, only the Hepburn rosy finch nests at these heights. "In the ledges of lava, jutting from the snow fields far above the timber line, this bird makes its home."[13]

At timberline—not a line at all, but a transition belt between about 6,000 feet and 8,000 feet above sea level—continuous forest growth gives way first to forest-enclosed meadows and then to open, rocky stretches of prostrate, wind-whipped shrubs and gnarled conifers Germans call **krummholz** or "crooked wood."

The principal tree throughout this belt is the mountain hemlock that dominates the extensive, park-like plateaus around the bases of the Three Sisters and Broken Top. Almost pure stands of fully-grown mountain hemlocks occupy some sites. On others, the tree alternates with clumps of alpine fir, whitebark pine and lodgepole pine interspersed with grassy meadows and pumice flats graced by wild-flowers—blue lupine and red paintbrush and a plethora of other colorful species—and Newberry's knotweed during the short summers. There are, of course, many variations on this theme. Around the Green

Lakes, for example, extensive areas of white pumice support a fragile vegetation of sparse grasses, alpine flowers, and the ubiquitous knotweed, and higher hummocks and ridges contain clusters of mountain hemlock, fir, and whitebark pine. Four miles to the south-west, groves of mountain hemlock and lodgepole pine dot the large, pumice-strewn Wickiup Plain, otherwise covered by knotweed and sparse bunchgrasses. The largest mountain hemlock in Oregon is thought to stand along Fall Creek about two miles downstream from the Green Lakes. At higher elevations, all these trees assume a semi-pros-trate form; there, along with creeping juniper, they cling to rock and life before they disappear at about 8,000 feet. Below the mountain hemlock forest, the mostly barren lava flows support an occasional whitebark pine, penstemon, or parsley fern, and lodgepole pines dominate many sites. In the lower, northeastern reaches of the region, extensive lodge-pole pine forests transition into lower elevation ponderosa pine forests.

Deer and elk are the most common large mammals in the Alpine Crest Region, where black bear, mountain lion, and coyote also spend at least part of the year. Mule deer and their close cousins, black-tailed deer, browse mainly on shrubs in the timberline belt and below during the summer months. For the winter, the mule deer migrate eastward toward the High Desert while the black-tailed deer move westward into the lower elevations of the McKenzie River and its tributaries. Elk herds summer in the region, where they eat grasses and broadleaf herbs, then move downslope and often outside the wilderness for the winter. Mountain lions, locally called cougar, range widely through all but the highest parts of the region to prey on deer and elk as well as smaller mammals including rabbits, squirrels, and mice. Coyotes, present in the high country but more common at lower elevations, pursue a varied diet that may include an occasional young or sick deer but emphasizes smaller mammals, birds, amphibians, reptiles, fish, insects and berries. Black bears, which enjoy a wide variety of plant foods, are common if not often seen. Also present are many smaller mammals such as marten, badger, and weasel. Native lynx and wolverine may remain.

During the summer, the region's meadows are alive with chipmunks, golden-mantled ground squirrels, gophers, mice, and shrews. Especially interesting is the little pika, described by Hodge as a "little beast"

who spends the greater part of his life beneath the lava, coming out for a short period during the summer months. He is the very soul of industry. No sooner does the snow melt than the little fellow is out looking for the first tender shoots of alpine plants or grass. These are cut and piled in the sun to dry. As soon as the "hay" is thoroughly cured, it is carried beneath the lava ledges and stored for use during the long months of winter.[14]

Since the pika doesn't hibernate, these "haypiles" are vital to winter survival. Yellow-bellied marmots, sometimes called "whistlers" for their unique call, also inhabit alpine lava flows where they forage through the summer and hibernate through the winter.

Predatory birds include the bald eagle and a variety of hawks. The ubiquitous Clarks nutcrackers are

among the largest mountain birds, conspicuous by their noisy calls, and the striking black and white plumage of their wings. Because they feed on the soft green cones of the white-bark pines, the gray feathers on their heads and throats are often stained a brilliant purple by the sap from the cones.[15]

A plethora of other fascinating birds—blackbirds, bluebirds, chickadees, crossbills, dippers, goshawks, hummingbirds, jays, juncos, sapsuckers, siskins, sparrows, woodpeckers, and others common and rare—rounds out the region's avian population.

Natural fish populations retreated as Ice Age glaciers advanced, and later were able to reach only those lakes formed by glacial and volcanic activity to which they could swim. Since most Alpine Crest Region streams that drain some of these lakes include impassable waterfalls, the lakes contain no natural fish populations. Those that now hold fish, essentially the Green Lakes, are artificially stocked with brook and rainbow trout. Most other lakes in the region, including Moraine Lake and the twentieth-century moraine-dam lakes, cannot support fish life and are not stocked.

The Lower Crest Region. The southeastern third of the Three Sisters Wilderness, an area of moderate relief where elevations range from about 4,900 feet to 6,839 feet above sea level, is an upland on which the High Cascades crest is not well defined. Indeed, the Lower Crest Region, with only an occasional small butte or low mountain, seems more like a plateau than a dividing range. Thickly forested with occasional meadows, it is a gently rolling land of volcanic depressions and glacially-scoured basins filled with many lakes. An abundance of summer mosquitoes and a shortage of distant views somewhat limit visitation to this part of the wilderness.

Topography. As its name implies, the Lower Crest region is part of the High Cascades crest that is lower than and not surmounted by the lofty, snow-capped volcanoes that characterize the Alpine Crest Region. Here the overlapping shield volcanoes of the High Cascades Platform, studded by occasional small, sometimes glaciated volcanic

Numerous small, unnamed lakes and small, glaciated volcanic buttes are found in the Lower Crest Region of the Three Sisters Wilderness.

mountains and cinder cones that rarely rise more than 1,500 feet above the surrounding terrain, define a much less spectacular upland divide between east and west. From north to south, **Red Hill** (6,250 feet) and **Horse Mountain** (6,224 feet) rise about 1,200 feet above Horse Lake Basin; Horse Mountain along with **Packsaddle Mountain** (6,138 feet) and **Williamson Mountain** (6,304 feet) rise similarly to surround larger Mink Lake Basin. **Little Round Top Mountain** (6,114 feet) and the region's highest, **Irish Mountain** (6,891 feet), mark the crest southward to the wilderness boundary. Otherwise, the landscape is the "gently rolling land of volcanic depressions and glacially-scoured basins" described previously. The porous soils are usually fine to coarse air-fall pumice or glacial till associated with rugged lava flows.

Hydrography. One of the Pacific Northwest's larger concentrations of small lakes and lakelets is found in the Lower Crest Region. Major surface streams are absent, but there is abundant subsurface drainage through very permeable volcanic soils and rocks. The region's many small, short, seasonal streams flow from springs into these lakes and lakelets that are often grouped in basins that lack surface stream outlets. Marshes are also present. Many of these lakes, lakelets, and marshes occupy irregular depressions on lava surfaces, and many of these have been modified by glacial activity. Indeed, it is often difficult to determine which factor, volcanism or glaciation, was dominant in the formation of any particular lake or group of lakes.

Sisters Mirror Lake (14 acres, 10 feet deep) is the largest and most easterly of a cluster of small lakes and ponds nestled on the crest at 6,000 feet between House Rock, Burnt Top, and Koosah Mountain in the transition zone between the Alpine Crest and Lower Crest regions. Three miles to the southeast and a thousand feet lower, **Horse Lake** (60 acres, 24 feet deep), easily recognized by the rocky peninsula that juts from its western shore, is the largest in the broad **Horse Lake Basin** that **Horse Creek** drains toward the northwest into the McKenzie River.

Lakes are more numerous in the large **Mink Lake Basin**, a few miles to the south and at about the same elevation, than anywhere else in the Three Sisters Wilderness. **Mink Lake** (180 acres, 70 feet deep), the largest in this wilderness and Oregon's second largest wilderness lake (Marion Lake in the Mt. Jefferson Wilderness, 360 acres in size and three times as deep, is the largest), is relatively deep and has very little shallow water. It is surrounded by a dozen or so smaller, forest-rimmed lakes—of which **Mac Lake** (70 acres, 42 feet deep), **Porky Lake** (60 acres, 19 feet deep), **Corner Lake** (60 acres, 14 feet deep), and **Junction Lake** (50 acres, 17 feet deep) are the larger—and dozens of smaller lakes, lakelets, and ponds. Striations on the ridge on the western side of **Cliff Lake** (40 acres, 24 feet deep), just east of Porky Lake and one of the region's prettier lakes, are evidence that glaciers gouged out its cliff-surrounded bed.

To the east, between the Mink Lake Basin and the Cascade Lakes Highway, deep blue **Doris Lake** (90 acres, 71 feet deep) is the solitary occupant of a small, glacially-scoured basin. Since no perennial surface streams flow into or out of the lake, it is presumed filled and drained by seepage. Just to the east is **Blow Lake** (55 acres, 23 feet deep), and three miles south on the other side of Williamson Mountain is **Lucky Lake** (30 acres, 52 feet deep).

South of the Mink Lake Basin is a chain of several lakes more or less anchored by **Winopee Lake** (40 acres, 43 feet deep) which "is perhaps more marsh than lake" since only about a third of its surface is "open water, unobstructed by emerging macrophytes."[16] The lake is deepest toward its northern end, and two long, marshy arms reach to the south. The largest of several small surface streams that flow into Winopee Lake flows out of rock-rimmed **Snowshoe Lake** (18 acres, 15 feet deep) just to the north. A sluggish stream that flows from

Winopee Lake, Three Sisters Wilderness

Winopee Lake's southeastern arm reaches **Muskrat Lake** (10 acres, 17 feet deep), a small, shallow body of water rapidly becoming a marsh, before flowing into Cultus Lake south of the wilderness boundary. North of the Snowshoe Lakes the chain includes diminutive Long and Puppy lakes, and southeast of Muskrat Lake are larger North Teddy and South Teddy lakes.

Finally, extending southward along the High Cascades crest from the Mink Lake Basin and Packsaddle Mountain to **Irish Lake** (28 acres, 16 feet deep) on the wilderness boundary, is a string of lakes that, in its southern reaches, merges with the Many Lakes Basin just inside the wilderness west of Cultus Mountain. The more significant of these lakes, descending in elevation from north to south from 6,400 feet to 5,500 feet, are **McFarland Lake** (39 acres, 54 feet deep) on the western flank of the crest, East McFarland Lake just about on the crest, Lindick Lake and Dennis Lake on the eastern flank of the crest, little Stormy Lake and aptly-named Rock Rim Lake at the eastern foot of Irish Mountain, and Brahma Lake. Then, to the east, in the **Many Lakes Basin**, late, light glaciation scoured dozens of small, closed depressions occupied by small lakes and ponds at about 5,500 feet above sea level. Among these, all but two smaller than 15 acres and most less than 15 feet deep, are East Hanks Lake, Middle Hanks Lake, and West Hanks Lake, and the much smaller Harlequin Lake, Phantom Lake, Kershaw Lake, Kinnikinnik Lake, and Merle Lake.

Flora and Fauna. Except for the absence of some species that live at or above timberline and the presence of some species that inhabit its lower stream and lake habitats, the flora and fauna of the Lower Crest Region are quite similar to those of the Alpine Crest Region.

Mountain hemlock and lodgepole pine are the dominant trees. Mountain hemlock occupies north-facing slopes and higher elevations while lodgepole pine is found at lower elevations and within old burns in the mountain hemlock forest. At lower elevations and on wetter sites, the lodgepole pines are typically associated with relatively lush under-stories of sedges and grasses mixed with numerous forbs, huckleberries and blueberries, and occasional quaking aspen and Englemann spruce. Bitterbrush and some ponderosa pine are found on some dryer sites. As the elevation increases, squaw current and bitterbrush are common, and the transition to a mountain hemlock forest begins. The mountain hemlock is variously associated with sedges, woodrushes, beargrass, and pinemat manzanita common on or near rock outcrops. Lupine is the most common of many wildflowers that grow in both forests.

Elk, deer, black bear, cougar, coyote, and smaller mammals are present throughout the region, as are amphibians—especially little tree frogs—and reptiles. Beaver and other riparian mammals are limited by the general lack of surface streams. Birds include the usual predators and others similar to those found in the other regions.

Most of the water bodies in the Lower Crest Region, the fairly recent products of glacial and volcanic activity and isolated from other waters by a lack of surface streams, did not contain historic native fish populations. Winopee Creek, Winopee Lake, and Muskrat Lake, inhabited by native trout and whitefish, were exceptions. The fish populations that now exist in many of the region's lakes are the result of twentieth-century artificial stocking by the Oregon Department of Fish and Wildlife with the assistance of the Forest Service and volunteer groups. Some of these populations reproduce, but others must be restocked to maintain the fishery. While a few lakes hold cutthroat or rainbow trout, brook trout predominate.

The Western Plateaus and Canyons Region. The western third of the Three Sisters Wilderness is a rugged region of moderate to steep relief where elevations range from about 1,850 feet to 7,524 feet above sea level. This forested plateau is deeply incised by glacially-gouged, foggy stream canyons, separated in their lower reaches by intervening steep ridges. Dominated by magnificent Douglas-fir forests at lower elevations and mountain hemlock forests at higher elevations, the Western Plateaus and Canyons Region is punctuated by remnant volcanoes, spotted by occasional lakes, and cut by twisting canyons.

Topography. The landscape of the Western Plateaus and Canyons Region, where elevations descend from about 6,000 feet above sea level at the base of the Three Sisters to about 1,850 feet at the western mouths of its canyons, belongs to both Cascade Ranges. While the relatively mild topography of the region's westerly-sloping plateaus is of the High Cascades Platform, the rugged series of deep canyons and sharp ridges that characterizes its western reaches is of the older Western Cascades.

The broad, gently-sloping volcanic plateaus in the eastern half of the region are topped by remnants of ancient volcanoes and incised by some of its major canyons and the upper reaches of others. **The Husband**, at 7,524 feet the highest mountain in the region, is the glaciated remains of a Pliocene volcano that helped build the High Cascades Platform. According to Williams:

The flows from this volcano, being impeded in their eastward spread by the ancestral [High Cascades], moved mainly in the opposite direction, and their fluidity was such that many of them poured...until they reached the border of the Western Cascades. In this direction they accumulated to thicknesses of more than 2,000 feet, as may be seen in the deep glacial canyons of Linton and Separation creeks.[17]

"It must not be supposed, however, that this vast succession of flows escaped solely from the central crater of [The Husband]," Williams continued. Rather, "many lavas issued from subsidiary vents far down the sides of the shield. Two of these contributing sources lay close to Proxy and Substitute Points."[18] Thus, both **Proxy Point** (6,203 feet) and **Substitute Point** (6,344 feet), about two miles west of The Husband, seem to be remains of Pliocene volcanoes.

Williams interpreted **The Wife** (7,054 feet), just west of Rock Mesa, as the largest of another group of Pliocene volcanoes—that includes **Sphinx Butte** (6,455 feet), **Burnt Top** (6,325 feet), and possibly **Koosah Mountain** (6,520 feet)—that added flows that built the platform as far north as those from The Husband, as far south as Horse Lake, and westward to the margin of the Western Cascades.

Ice Age glaciers later gutted The Husband and eroded the other volcanoes as they carved the deep canyons of Linton and Separation

The Wife, Three Sisters Wilderness

creeks. "The glacier that...occupied Nash Lake Canyon obliterated most of the north part of [Burnt Top], and had it cut back a little farther it would have exposed the central conduit."[19]

Other glaciers advanced off the plateau and into stream valleys of the Western Cascades to gouge the series of deep canyons and sharp ridges in the western part of the region where erosion is much farther advanced. Here, **Sawtooth Ridge** (4,800 feet) and the ridges of **Yankee Mountain** (5,430 feet), **Olallie Mountain** (5,700 feet), **Pyramid Mountain** (5,590 feet), **Rebel Rock** (5,600 feet) and others rise thousands of feet above the streams that drain their slopes into the South Fork of the McKenzie River.

Hydrography. Most of the major surface streams in the Three Sisters Wilderness drain the well-watered Western Plateaus and Canyons Region. This region, also, is characterized by extensive percolation through porous watersheds and lakes that are few and far between.

Originating on the western slopes of the Three Sisters and in the western lake basins of the Lower Crest Region, many tributaries of the McKenzie River flow into and through the deep, river-cut and glacier-carved canyons that incise the plateaus of the western third of the wilderness.

Proxy Falls, Three Sisters Wilderness

At the region's northern end, a lava flow from Collier Cone and Four-in-One Cone down the canyon of one of those tributaries, **White Branch Creek**, dammed two of its tributaries, **Linton Creek** and **Obsidian Creek**, to create solitary **Linton Lake** (50 acres, 90 feet deep), the largest in the region. A few miles upstream, Obsidian Creek plunges over beautiful, 20-foot **Obsidian Falls** shortly after it rises from springs due west of North Sister, while Linton Creek rises in springs surrounding Linton Meadows, between Middle Sister and The Husband. Not two miles west of Linton Lake, **Proxy Creek,** another White Branch Creek tributary, flows out of a canyon flanked by The Husband and Proxy Point to drop 200 feet off a lava plateau in two distinct cascades at **Proxy Falls**.

Separation Creek, **Horse Creek**, **Eugene Creek**, **French Pete Creek**, and **Rebel Creek** occupy the region's main canyons as they flow northwesterly or westerly toward the McKenzie River several thousand feet below their headwaters. Other significant water features in the heart of the region are **Honey Lake** (15 acres, 37 feet deep) and about a dozen smaller lakes and lakelets in its group southeast of Substitute Point, and lonely **Nash Lake** (33 acres, 34 feet deep) just north of Burnt Top.

In the southwestern end of this region, the **Erma Bell Lakes** occupy glacier-scoured pockets at elevations of 4,500 feet to 4,800 feet above sea level just east of the deep canyon of the Middle Fork of the Willamette River. **Lower Erma Bell Lake** (55 acres, 60 feet deep) is a rock-rimmed, circular lake into which water tumbles 100 feet from **Middle Erma Bell Lake** (60 acres, 46 feet deep) just 200 yards south. Less than half a mile south and 200 feet higher in elevation, **Upper Erma Bell Lake** (25 acres, 30 feet deep) receives flow from much smaller Mud Lake. Two small creeks, one draining Lower Erma Bell Lake and the other draining **Otter Lake** (17 acres, 27 feet deep) just to the north, supplement subsurface flow into the Middle Fork.

Flora and Fauna. One of the larger remaining old-growth Douglas-fir forests in the nation is preserved in the lower western drainages of the Western Plateaus and Canyons Region at elevations between about 1,850 and 3,500 feet above sea level. Here, where the giant of Pacific Northwest trees attains awesome ages and sizes, countless Douglas-firs that exceed 200 feet in height and eight feet in diameter thrive in a relatively mild and moist climate. In the region's lower elevations, Douglas-fir comprises most of the forest, sometimes in pure or almost pure stands, sometimes associated with western hemlock,

Douglas-fir forest, Three Sisters Wilderness

and sometimes intermingled with grand fir, incense and western red cedars, and western hemlock. The lush ground cover is replete with salal, sword ferns, huckleberries, Oregon grape, rhododendron, and various other species; the understory features yew, dogwood, vine maple, bigleaf maple along streams as well as on dryer sites, and madrone on dry sites. A diverse population of wildflowers includes vanilla leaf, violets, coral-root orchids, and wintergreens. In addition to the higher plants, fungi, mosses, liverworts, and lichens abound.

On some western ridges, such as Sawtooth Ridge and Yankee Mountain, the forest differs from that in the intervening stream canyons as well as from that at the same elevation and slope exposure farther east in the region. Here, no lodgepole pine is found; instead, the true firs and hemlocks dominate, and a few western white pine, whitebark pine, and scraggly Douglas-fir grow. Open, grassy areas occur on south-facing slopes.

As the elevation increases eastward, the Douglas-fir gradually yields dominance to western hemlock at about 3,500 feet, and this tree is mixed with lodgepole pine, true firs, western white pine, and, in wet places, Englemann spruce. Additional variety is provided by occasional openings such as Quaking Aspen Swamp, Cedar Swamp, Wildcat Swamp, and Cow Swamp that break the almost continuous forest. These island habitats are important to elk and other wildlife. Higher still, mountain hemlock becomes dominant as the region approaches the High Cascades crest and merges with the other Three Sisters Wilderness regions. At the higher elevations on the western edge of the region, especially around The Husband and some of the other old volcanic peaks, the vegetation approximates that of the adjacent Alpine Crest Region. Just east of The Husband, grassy Linton Meadows is one of the larger breaks in this densely forested region.

Animals and birds are not as abundant in these forests as in other wilderness habitats. Herds of elk and black-tailed deer that summer in the Alpine Crest and Lower Crest regions move west to winter in the lower, warmer, forested canyons and valleys where the deer, especially, add Douglas-fir and western hemlock needles to their diet. These trees, indeed, feed many animals. "The seedlings are a winter staple for deer and hares, and the seeds are eaten by small birds and rodents. Bears sometimes strip the bark to eat its inner layer...."[20] Omnivorous black bears find a wide variety of other foods. Mountain lions and coyotes are present, as are the smaller mammals that flesh out their diets. American and mountain beaver, river otters, and the rare fisher inhabit riparian areas. A wide variety of birds lives in the region, as do salamanders, frogs, lizards, snakes, and insects. Natural trout populations are found in the tributaries of the McKenzie River which drain the region, but most of the region's few lakes were devoid of fish populations before the State of Oregon began its fish stocking program in the early 1900s.

Cultural History

The cultural history of the Three Sisters country is one of sequential visitation since the Ice Age by Native Americans followed in the last 150 years or so by Euro-American explorers, exploiters, and land managers who sought use of its varied amenity and commodity resources. It is not a history of sequential occupation, however, because the severe winters of the High Cascades have generally precluded permanent habitation or settlement. The country that became the Three Sisters Wilderness has almost always been, in the words of the Wilderness Act of 1964, an area "where man himself is a visitor who does not remain."

Native American Visitation and Utilization. Native Americans, especially the **Northern Paiute** of the High Desert to the east and the **Molalla** of the Western Cascades foothills, were the first human beings known to have visited and used the lands now included in the Three Sisters Wilderness. Instead of occupying this high country permanently, they visited seasonally to avail themselves of a variety of its resources. Autumn camps were especially popular. From these camps, they accessed the high country via game trails and water courses to pick huckleberries, hunt deer and other game, collect obsidian for arrowheads and spearheads as well as for trade, and gathered beargrass for basketry. Rock art left by these peoples, such as the pictographs still visible on the Devils Hill flow on the wilderness boundary north of the Cascade Lakes Highway, indicates that the country's peaks and lakes held spiritual meaning.

Although they left few marks other than faint trails and scattered obsidian chips on this land, the Native Americans did leave names for many of its features. Many of these names are in Chinook jargon, an Indian trading language. *Olallie*, for example, which means "berry," is the name of a mountain, a creek, and a meadow—and, later, a Forest Service guard station and fire lookout—in the western Three Sisters Wilderness. *Tipsoo*, given to a butte east of Cougar Reservoir, means "grassy." In the eastern part of the wilderness, the name for Koosah

Mountain south of the Mirror Lakes means "sky" and that for Kokostick Butte west of Devils Lake means "woodpecker." Some of these and many other names were applied by the Native Americans, and some later by Euro-American explorers and pioneers.

Euro-American Discovery and Exploration. Next to approach the Three Sisters country were European and Euro-American explorers who may or may not actually have entered the area. **Lewis and Clark** passed too far to the north to see the Three Sisters in 1805. But, twenty years later in 1825, **Peter Skene Ogden** of the Hudson's Bay Company reported "a number of lofty mountains" south of Mt. Hood—certainly the Three Sisters. Ten months later, in 1836, Scottish botanist **David Douglas** reported seeing the same peaks "covered with snow, in an unknown tract of country"[21] from the Willamette Valley. As that valley began to be settled in the 1840s, Euro-Americans began to approach the Three Sisters country from the west. During this time, members of a Methodist mission at Salem called the trio of peaks the Three Sisters and referred to them individually—from north to south—as Faith, Hope, and Charity. Meanwhile, explorers east of the Cascade Range, including **Nathaniel J. Wyeth** in 1839, **Captian John C. Fremont** at the head of a U.S. Army Topographic Corps expedition in 1843, and members of the Pacific Railroad Survey of 1855 led by **Lieutenant R. L. Williamson** and **Lieutenant Henry L. Abbot** and accompanied by **Dr. John Strong Newberry**, used the Three Sisters as visual navigation landmarks. The peaks appeared as the Three Sisters on Preston's 1856 map of Oregon.

As settlers filled the Willamette Valley and, later in the nineteenth century, crossed the Cascade Range to occupy parts of Central Oregon, road building and livestock raising drew them into the Three Sisters high country. In 1862, to connect the Willamette Valley with the gold mining settlements in eastern Oregon and Idaho as well as with ranches developing in Central Oregon, **Felix and Marion Scott** blazed a trail wide enough for wagons through the northern reaches of what is now the Three Sisters Wilderness. This route, which became known as the **Scott Trail**, traversed the lava fields just north of Yapoah Crater and crossed the Cascade Divide over **Scott Pass** (over 6,000 feet above sea level) south of the present-day **McKenzie Pass** (5,325 feet) highway route. Travel across the Cascade Range on the Scott Trail continued until supplanted by an improved lower McKenzie Pass route early in the twentieth century. Today, remnants of the trail are part of the Three Sisters Wilderness trail system.

Euro-American Exploitation and Conservation. As the Euro-Americans who settled the lands east and west of the Cascade Range and brought Oregon into the United States in 1859 approached the Three Sisters country, they first exploited and later managed the natural resources—both amenity and commodity resources—they found there. The first major step in regulating use of these resources was taken in 1893 when President Grover Cleveland, exercising authority granted by Congress in the Forest Reserve Act of 1891, proclaimed the **Cascade Range Forest Reserve** in 1893. This 4,492,000-acre reserve, which embraced "the main ridge of the Cascades and a broad strip on either side,"[22] extended about 235 miles from the Columbia River almost to the California border, was 18 to 60 miles wide, and included the Three Sisters country. Although many stockmen, timber speculators, homesteaders, and others objected, this reserve stood.

Administration of the forest reserves was transferred from the General Land Office in the Department of the Interior to the new U.S. Forest Service in the Department of Agriculture by the Transfer Act of 1905. In 1907, the renamed **Cascade Forest Reserve** was again renamed the **Cascade National Forest**, and beginning in 1908 was split into smaller national forests. By 1908, the eastern Three Sisters country was part of the **Deschutes National Forest**, one of the national forests carved out of the Cascade National Forest, and the residual Cascade National Forest administered the western Three Sisters country. In 1934, the Cascade and Santiam national forests were combined in the **Willamette National Forest** which, since that year, has included the western Three Sisters country. Since 1905, Forest Service supervisors and rangers of these national forests have managed and protected the natural resources of the Three Sisters country.

Timber. Timber, usually the first forest resource to come to mind, and water were the two principal resources the forest reserves were established in 1891 to protect. This resource has not been extensively harvested within the current Three Sisters Wilderness. Most of the commercially valuable timberlands now within the wilderness boundaries, including one of the largest remaining old-growth Douglas-fir forests in the nation, were either too remote for or not yet sought by commercial timber interests before the process to set those lands aside for amenity values rather than manage them for commodity production began. Other timberlands lacked commercial value. As described in Chapter One, however, the demand for timber during the third quarter of the twentieth century did affect establishment of past and present Three Sisters Wilderness boundaries.

It wasn't until after World War II, when much of the private timber in the Pacific Northwest had been cut, that more remote stands of national forest timber—including Willamette National Forest lands now within Three Sisters Wilderness boundaries—were "eagerly sought by an expanding Pacific Northwest timber industry."[23] This demand resulted in the 1957 decision to exclude low-elevation forests of commercial value west of Horse Creek from the Three Sisters Wilderness Area when its predecessor, the Three Sisters Primitive Area, was reclassified, and in the two-decade French Pete Creek controversy. Passage of the Endangered Wilderness Act of 1978 restored 45,400 acres of these disputed, excluded lands to the Three Sisters Wilderness, and generally settled the issue—if not the controversy— of including these commercially valuable forests within the wilderness. By the 1990s, a few inadvertent incursions that resulted in the cutting of timber just inside the wilderness boundaries remained the only apparent threat to the Three Sisters Wilderness posed by commercial timber operations.

Water. Water has been and remains the most precious resource the Three Sisters country and the rest of the Cascade Range contribute to the settled lands west and east of the mountains. The annual snowpack in the Three Sisters Wilderness, which includes significant headwaters of the McKenzie and Deschutes river systems, is a vital source of domestic, industrial, and agricultural water for the Willamette Valley and Central Oregon. Although efforts to increase use of Three Sisters country water have affected expansion of the Three Sisters Wilderness and once threatened wilderness values in the area, few if any conflicts between watershed and other wilderness benefits remain.

An early twentieth century **Tumalo Irrigation District** project to irrigate more lands northeast of Bend eventually affected eastward expansion of the Three Sisters Wilderness under the Oregon Wilderness Act of 1984. The plan to increase intake of Crater Creek and Soda Creek waters involved a two-mile canal to divert the flow of these creeks into the Middle Fork of Tumalo Creek and then via the Tumalo Feed Canal to the farm and ranch lands. Although waters diverted through **Crater Creek Ditch** have augmented the irrigation district's supply since 1916, the part of the plan to divert Soda Creek was not realized. The existence of Crater Creek Ditch diversion structures, however, prevented inclusion of much of Crater Creek's course in the Three Sisters Wilderness when the wilderness boundary was pushed eastward in 1984.

The quest for water to assure the survival of farming and ranching communities in other parts of Central Oregon spawned plans that, if carried out, would have prevented inclusion of some of the most popular and pristine places within the Three Sisters Wilderness. About 1912, for example, pioneer farmers and ranchers in the Plainview area east of Sisters wanted to channel waters from Camp Lake down the South Fork of Squaw Creek to the arid plains. The job, snowed out by an early fall storm, was abandoned. Then, in 1915, the Green Lakes Basin between South Sister and Broken Top was viewed by the **Squaw Creek Irrigation District** as a possible source of irrigation water for the arid lands near Plainview and Lower Bridge. A 20-foot-high dam at the southern end of the basin that would impound 7,500 acre-feet of water in the basin was proposed. A 6,335-foot tunnel through the divide north of the basin would convey this water into the Pole Creek and Squaw Creek drainages. Nothing was done to implement the $80,000 plan. Had such a project been constructed, however, the beautiful Green Lakes would have been significantly altered and could not have been included within the Three Sisters Wilderness. In a separate, unrealized proposal, when the city of Bend was looking for alternative water sources, Mayor R. L. Fox suggested that the city file a claim on the Green Lakes. Such water development schemes were dropped when the Three Sisters Primitive Area was established in 1937.

Forage. Forage was exploited early and extensively in the Three Sisters country. Wool and beef became important Oregon products during the 1860s, and much of it was grown east of the Cascade Range. As early as the 1870s, when Oregon sheepmen needed more summer range, sheep were driven toward the alpine ranges each spring. Dozens of bands of 1,500 to 2,500 sheep would enter the foothills in May or June, then move toward the higher elevations as the snow receded to reach the alpine meadows by August. Then, in September, before the storms set in, the herders would begin trailing their bands out of the high country.

In his 1898 report, *Forest Growth and Sheep Grazing in the Cascade Mountains of Oregon*, government botanist Frederick V. Coville described the two sheep grazing areas—which he called ranges—in what is now the Three Sisters Wilderness. In the Western Plateaus and Canyons Region, the "Horse Creek range" lay "on the headwaters of the McKenzie River...southwesterly from the Three Sisters. It consists of forest-covered mountain slopes and a large area of bottom land, the latter partly open meadow and partly forest." He described what he called the "Three Sisters range" as "lying near the crest of the Cascades…and extending chiefly down the eastern slope toward the head waters of Squaw Creek and Tumelow [sic] Creek. It is chiefly made up of natural meadows and old burns in lodgepole pine forests."[24] Some time later, and on a smaller scale, cattle were grazed on Three Sisters country ranges. By the 1890s, some of these ranges were seriously overgrazed.

From the time President Cleveland proclaimed the Cascade Range Forest Reserve in 1893, "there was a difference of opinion among the people of Oregon regarding the effect of sheep grazing within its limits, one party to the controversy maintaining that the sheep were a serious detriment to the interests for which the reserve was created, the other maintaining that they were not."[25] Among the opponents of sheep grazing in the reserve were recreational groups who valued the Three Sisters country and other parts of the reserve for their mountaineering as well as hunting and fishing outings. Many members of the Mazamas, Oregon's most prestigious mountaineering club, opposed sheep grazing. "There was also opposition from Indians and whites alike who utilized the huckleberry meadows, as the presence of sheep was considered incompatible with berry picking."[26] As a result, government regulations for all the forest reserves issued in April 1894 prohibited the "driving, feeding, grazing, pasturing, or herding of cattle, sheep, or other live stock"[27] within any of the reserves.

But the sheepmen were not to be denied. They protested their exclusion from the Cascade Range Forest Reserve to the Department of the Interior, the Congress, and the Oregon legislature. Several were arrested for illegally grazing sheep on the reserve. And they were up against big guns in the form of the 1896 National Academy of Sciences commission on forest reserves sent west to study their resources and to help "the inaguration of a national forest policy."[28] Its report reflected the opinion of member John Muir, who hated sheep.

The sheepmen's politicking, along with the results of Coville's summer 1897 investigation of Cascade Range Forest Reserve grazing published early in 1898, helped restore and regulate grazing on the reserve. First, Congress passed the Organic Administrative Act of 1897 that authorized the Secretary of the Interior to "make such rules and regulations" needed to administer the reserves, and the General Land Office issued regulations that permitted grazing on the reserve provided that no damage was done to forest growth. Coville's report, which detailed the effects and extent of overgrazing, and reported that overgrazing had decreased "the amount of pasturage afforded by particular ranges" including "a large portion of the range that lies immediately to the east of the Three Sisters,"[29] recommended grazing regulations based on the carrying capacity of the range. Coville's regulations, which recognized amenity values such as recreation as well as commodity values, were put into effect and, in the Three Sisters country, enforced by pioneer forest rangers including the legendary **Cy Bingham** in a way that led to generally harmonious cooperation between the grazers and the forest administrators. Although some cattle and horses were grazed, most of the stock grazed in the Three Sisters country was sheep.

Grazing peaked in the Three Sisters country about 1910, then began to fall off as a result of competing uses for the land—huckleberry harvesting, recreation along the Oregon Skyline Trail, and management of forage for deer and elk—and a decline in the grazing industry. On the Willamette National Forest side of the Three Sisters country, grazing allotments in the North Sister and Middle Sister areas were closed about 1932 or 1933, the area adjacent to the Skyline Trail was closed to grazing in 1938, and the allotments in the South Sister area were closed in 1944. Sheep grazing ended on the Deschutes National Forest side in 1932, when grazing was limited to cattle.

As early as 1916, Culver and Plainview area ranchers drove cattle along the eastern slopes of the Three Sisters to summer range at Sparks Lake meadow. These drives moved up Pole Creek to Park Meadow, then climbed toward the saddle between South Sister and Broken Top, passed by—and sometimes over the frozen—Green Lakes, and descended Fall Creek and crossed the Cascade Lakes Highway to the Sparks Lake allotment. The last of these drives occurred in 1963, when the McCoin and Holmes families drove about a hundred head of cattle to the Sparks Lake allotment, a year before Congress passed the Wilderness Act. Thereafter, the cattle were trucked around to the Sparks Lake allotment until it was closed in the 1990s.

All grazing in the Three Sisters Wilderness, except for that of recreational livestock on pack trips, ended in the 1990s.

Wildlife. Wildlife has been and remains a widely used Three Sisters country resource. Although trapping of fur-bearing animals for pelts and hunting of predators for bounties are things of the past, subsistence hunting as well as recreational hunting and fishing in accordance with State of Oregon fish and game laws remain important uses of the Three Sisters Wilderness. Visitors who don't hunt or fish appreciate viewing, photographing, and studying wildlife.

This cattle drive, en route a Deschutes National Forest grazing allotment near Sparks Lake, crossed the saddle north of the Green Lakes in the Three Sisters Primitive Area in 1949.

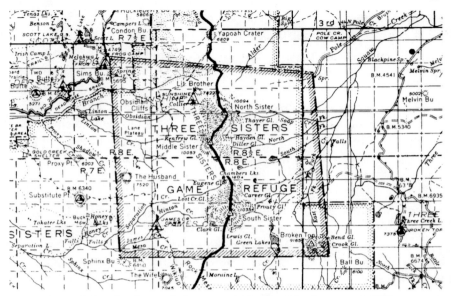

Designated by the State of Oregon within the Deschutes and Willamette national forests, the Three Sisters Game Refuge included the Three Sisters, Broken Top, and surrounding country from 1929 to 1955.

Early fur trapping in the latter two-thirds of the nineteenth century reduced many species in and around the Three Sisters country. Beaver populations were greatly decreased, and mink, marten, weasel, ermine, fisher, and wolverine populations were affected. Hunts to kill large numbers of wolves, grizzly bears, coyotes, mountain lions, and other predators were also common. The gray wolf and grizzly bear were extirpated, and mountain lion and coyote numbers were reduced.

The early years of wildlife management involved complex interaction between federal and state agencies. After 1905, the Forest Service managed the land—and the habitat—within the national forests, and the U.S. Bureau of Biological Survey (a forerunner of the modern U.S. Fish and Wildlife Service) accomplished wildlife research and some predator control. Administration of hunting and fishing, a "states' right" under the Constitution, fell to the Oregon State Game Commission. Forest Service rangers were appointed as deputy state game wardens with authority to enforce state fish and game laws. As early as 1913, the game commission enlisted the help of Forest Service packers in stocking Husband Lake and then other Three Sisters country lakes and streams with trout to promote sport fishing. Beginning in the 1920s, the Forest Service and the Biological Survey conducted an annual game census. In 1929, the State of Oregon established the Three Sisters Game

Refuge within the Cascade and Deschutes national forests "largely at the request of recreationists who objected to random shooting."[30]

Although trapping in the Three Sisters country declined as the idea of wilderness preservation began to take hold, the business left its mark at Muskrat Lake within the current Three Sisters Wilderness. There, in 1934, well known Central Oregon log cabin builder Luther Metke constructed a one-room cabin for Ted Wallace who wanted living quarters for trappers who were setting and maintaining trap lines to supply his muskrat farm. Wallace's muskrat farm failed, but his cabin—the last log cabin in the Three Sisters Wilderness—remains to tell the story.

As the science of wildlife management evolved, techniques such as predator control and game refuges intended to produce large deer and elk herds gave way to more enlightened methods that emphasized habitat management for sustainable populations of both game and non-game species. Predator control was largely abandoned, and the game refuge around the Three Sisters was disestablished in 1955. Today, Deschutes and Willamette national forest wildlife biologists cooperate closely with other federal and state agencies, university scientists, and national and local fish and wildlife groups to balance wildlife with other wilderness values.

Minerals. Commercially important mineral resources are generally lacking in the Three Sisters Wilderness, and—with one significant exception—mining has neither damaged nor posed a threat to wilderness values.

About 1961, the U.S. Pumice Company filed claims under the Mining Law of 1872, that declared "all valuable mineral deposits in lands belonging to the United States...free and open to exploration and purchase," on portions of Rock Mesa south of South Sister. The company planned to keep in business by mining this Three Sisters Wilderness Area property when its Mono Craters pumice supply near Lee Vining, California, was exhausted. Necessary access roads were built and improvements were made to maintain the claim. An environmental statement on the proposed mining of Rock Mesa prepared by the Deschutes National Forest in 1974 detailed the threat to the Three Sisters Wilderness:

This mining activity, though legal, would [be inconsistent with] the character of the wilderness. The quality of the wilderness experience would be reduced for the users in this area [by] the noise and sight of the trucks and equipment..., dust clouds from mining, and roads.... The appearance of the surface of Rock Mesa...would be altered. A considerable portion of this unique geological formation would be lost. Soils, vegetation, and some wildlife would be disturbed.[31]

Also, as the statement recognized, "that portion of the Pacific Crest Trail that now skirts the western edge of Rock Mesa" would have to be relocated "to avoid the mining area."[32] Finally, curious visitors would increase use, and that would add to the costs of administering the wilderness.

When, in 1974, the company's Rock Mesa claim was evaluated and determined valid, it became apparent that the claim would have to be bought out to end this threat to the integrity of the Three Sisters Wilderness. The questions of how much that would cost and who would pay the price were answered in 1982 when President Ronald Reagan signed the bill that permitted the U.S. Government to acquire the company's claim to Rock Mesa for two million dollars. Rock Mesa was preserved.

Recreation. The recreation resources of the Three Sisters country have been appreciated and enjoyed for centuries, and probably for millennia. Certainly the Native Americans who summered there found this High Cascades country physically and spiritually refreshing. As the Willamette Valley and, later, Central Oregon, were settled, late nineteenth and early twentieth century mountaineers seeking challenge and others seeking respite from town and city life availed themselves of its amenities. Many in those towns and cities, of course, saw development of this recreation resource as an economic boon to their communities. Others saw a wilderness to preserve. Their efforts to work with the U.S. Government to administer this resource ran the gamut from developing extensive tourist accommodations and facilities, on the one hand, to wilderness preservation, on the other. Throughout the twentieth century, use and protection of the recreation and other resources of the Three Sisters country have brought development of access routes and administrative practices and facilities that remain part of the Three Sisters Wilderness scene and story.

Access. Early visitors reached the Three Sisters country by trails and primitive roads that led to trailheads east and west of the High Cascades crest. The high country itself was "traversed by a network of trails, some of them made by Indians crossing from the east side of the mountains to the west, some built by pioneers or prospectors, some pioneered by early Forest Service men...."[33] Eventually, as automobiles replaced stagecoaches (an account of a 1903 ascent of the

Three Sisters mentioned a day-long trip by stage from Eugene to McKenzie Bridge), primitive motor roads crossed passes north and south of the Three Sisters country and improved access to the region.

About 1920, visionary Forest Service officer **Fred W. Cleator**, responsible for planning and developing recreation facilities on Pacific Northwest national forests, moved on proposals to build a road and a trail along the High Cascades crest from Mt. Hood—and through the Three Sisters country—to Crater Lake.

The advent of the automobile had made scenic mountain highways popular. Encouraged by the Oregon Chamber of Commerce and local boosters after tourism dollars, Cleator planned a 200-mile-long **Oregon Skyline Road** that would cost about $2.5 million to build. Resorts, campgrounds, and even aircraft landing strips were planned. The road would "open these almost unknown scenic attractions to tourist travel and human enjoyment,"[34] a booklet called *The Oregon Skyline Road* claimed, and would attract business to the region.

Cleator examined the proposed route for the road during a 1920 summer pack trip from Crater Lake to Mt. Jefferson that took him through the Three Sisters country. He "took with him a large number of trail markers and signs" and, when he posted them, "the **Oregon Skyline Trail** was officially born."[35] The proposed road would run west of the trail.

The prohibitive cost of the Skyline Road—and, perhaps, growing interest in wilderness preservation—prevented construction. But construction of the Skyline Trail, much less expensive and much more compatible with wilderness values, continued during the 1920s and into the 1930s. In 1931, the North Pacific Region of the Forest Service published a detailed *Oregon Skyline Trail Map* folder that, among other things, described access to the Three Sisters country by "fairly good automobile road" from Eugene and Bend. By 1933, Cleator could report completion of "the Crater Lake-Mt. Hood section...to a fairly good safe high standard route," and in 1936 he reported the trail had been "provided with about 85 campgrounds and some 35 rustic shelters."[36] Three of these 1934 shelters remain in the Three Sisters Wilderness at James Creek, Mink Lake, and Cliff Lake. "Walking with a back pack," according to the map folder, was "the simplest, though slowest and most tiring way" to travel the trail. "Horses, mules, or burros with packs will give the most satisfaction."[37] Pack trips were popular, and pack stations such as the one at Elk Lake for several decades outfitted and guided trips into the Three Sisters country and along the Skyline Trail.

Forest Service official Fred W. Cleator pioneered and posted the Oregon Skyline Trail—later incorporated into the Pacific Crest National Scenic Trail—in 1920.

Cliff Lake Shelter, built along the Oregon Skyline Trail in 1934, remains in the Three Sisters Wilderness.

In the 1960s, as backpacking began to appeal to large numbers of people, the federal Bureau of Outdoor Recreation recommended establishment of a national system of trails. Congress passed the National Trails System Act of 1968, and the Oregon Skyline Trail was incorporated into the **Pacific Crest National Scenic Trail** that now extends 2,638 miles from Canada to Mexico. About 50 miles of this famed trail, also called the "Pacific Crest Trail" or just the "PCT," are the spine of the Three Sisters Wilderness trail system. The trail enters the wilderness at McKenzie Pass in the north, passes through the Alpine Crest Region on the western side of the Three Sisters, and transits the Lower Crest Region lake basins before exiting at Irish Lake.

Another 200 or so miles of maintained "system trails" flesh out the Three Sisters Wilderness transportation system as they provide access to the Pacific Crest Trail and to most principal destinations within the wilderness. In the Alpine Crest Region, the popular trail up Fall Creek to the Green Lakes continues northward along the eastern slope of the Three Sisters toward McKenzie Pass, and lateral trails provide access to Moraine Lake, the Broken Top area, the Chambers Lakes area, and other destinations. Another popular trail ascends South Sister, and still another provides easy access to the Wickiup Plain and the Pacific Crest Trail. Trails thread their way through the lake basins of the

More visitors—about 45 percent of the total—approach the Three Sisters Wilderness via the Cascade Lakes Highway than by any other route. This highway connects the rapidly-growing Bend area with the wilderness.

Lower Crest Region and progress up the forested canyons and across the plateaus of the Western Plateaus and Canyons Region.

Three paved highways—among the first fifty National Forest Scenic Byways in the nation—and a few lesser paved and unpaved roads provide access to 55 trailheads at which trails enter the Three Sisters Wilderness and beyond which travel is by foot or on horseback. In the west, trails from about a dozen trailheads along the **Robert Aufderheide Memorial Drive** (Forest Route 19) penetrate the lush Douglas-fir forest of the Walker, French Pete, Rebel, and lesser creeks en route the high country. In the north, the Pacific Crest Trail and other trails depart another dozen or so trailheads along or just off the scenic **McKenzie Pass Highway** (Oregon Highway 242) for Black Crater, the Three Sisters, the Obsidian area, Linton Lake, Linton Meadows and The Husband, Proxy Falls, and other destinations. Deschutes National Forest roads south of Highway 242 lead to another half dozen trailheads that afford access to the wilderness from the northeast. More visitors approach the Three Sisters Wilderness from the east via the **Cascade Lakes Highway** (Forest Route 46) than by any other route, and access the most popular parts of the wilderness at the Green Lakes Trailhead and about a dozen others from which trails lead up South Sister and into

Forest guards like Ralph Heath (right), shown here with District Ranger Ray Engles of the Willamette National Forest's McKenzie Ranger District in July 1939, patrolled the Three Sisters Primitive Area from Horse Lake Guard Station, built in 1933 and removed in 1972.

the Broken Top area, Moraine Lake, the Wickiup Plain, and the Lower Crest region lake basins. Relatively few enter from the south via trailheads off rugged Forest Route 600.

Administration. The recreation resources—as well as the other natural resources—of the Three Sisters country have been administered by the Forest Service since 1905. Early forest rangers were, for the most part, custodians who regulated grazing, fought fires, enforced fish and game laws, helped stock lakes with trout, built and maintained trails, and dealt with conflicts between recreation and other resource uses. District rangers posted seasonal assistants, called forest guards, in the high country, and in 1933 the Willamette National Forest built **Olallie Guard Station** and **Horse Lake Guard Station** from which they worked. Also, fire lookouts were built and staffed atop Black Crater in 1925 and on Tam McArthur Rim in 1931 by the Deschutes National Forest, and atop Olallie Mountain in 1932, Substitute Point in 1933, Tipsoo Butte in 1934, Packsaddle Mountain in 1936, and Rebel Rock in 1955 by the Willamette National Forest—all within the current Three Sisters Wilderness—for wildfire detection. All these fire lookouts were out of service by the late 1960s; however, the Olallie and

Rebel Rock structures remain. Horse Lake Guard Station was removed in 1972, and the Olallie Guard Station was demolished when two large Douglas-firs fell on it during a 1997 windstorm. Throughout its years as a primitive area and wilderness area, the Three Sisters country was patrolled and protected by a combination of recreation and fire guards. Today, wilderness rangers patrol and maintain the trails and smoke jumpers attack remote fires.

Throughout much of the twentieth century, as visitors enjoyed the Three Sisters country in ever increasing numbers, others struggled with how and by whom this land should be administered. Sometimes timber and other commodity interests conflicted with recreational use—a primary concern of surrounding chambers of commerce and outdoor clubs—or with growing pressure for wilderness preservation. Many alternatives to Forest Service administration were proposed. Between 1922 and 1927, for example, a **Three Sisters National Park** was promoted by a Three Sisters Club in Bend and commercial interests in Eugene, but no bill was introduced in Congress. This early national park effort failed for several reasons. One of these was "agency territorial protection. The Forest Service did not want to lose its lands for national park creation"[38] as it had in the Grand Canyon in 1919.

Sometimes east and west failed to agree on such proposals. While, in 1934, interests in Bend were pushing for a **Three Sisters National Monument** to attract national attention and "to draw travel from the Willamette Highway north through Bend,"[39] citizens in Eugene were "more interested in a primitive area...than a monument."[40] As described in Chapter One, the Three Sisters Primitive Area was designated in the Deschutes and Willamette national forests in 1937, and the Three Sisters Wilderness Area was established in 1957. The wilderness concept had gained the upper hand.

As the battle over the wilderness bill raged in Congress, the Sierra Club proposed a **Cascades Volcanic National Park** in 1959. This park would include the Three Sisters Wilderness Area along with the Mt. Washington Wild Area and Mt. Jefferson Primitive Area, to the north, and the Diamond Peak Wild Area and Waldo Lake, to the south. A similar **Oregon Volcanoes National Park** was proposed in 1960. These proposals, however, were opposed in Central Oregon in favor of continued Forest Service administration and doomed by competition to carve the North Cascades National Park out of national forests in Washington. Then, in 1964, passage of the Wilderness Act created the Three Sisters Wilderness.

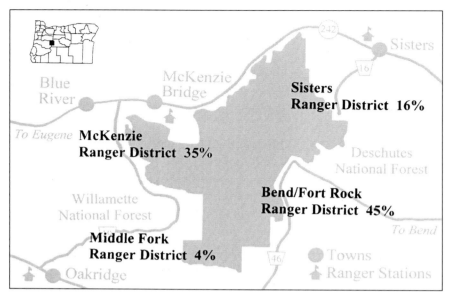

About three-fifths of the visitors use occurs on the one third of the Three Sisters Wilderness managed by the Bend/Fort Rock and Sisters ranger districts of the Deschutes National Forest.

In 1971, as the dispute over including the French Pete Creek area in the Three Sisters Wilderness raged, both Senator Bob Packwood and Representative Edith Green introduced bills in Congress to create a national recreation area there. Neither bill passed, and the issue was resolved when the Endangered Wilderness Act of 1978 added the area to the wilderness.

Also in 1971, as concern that "the Three Sisters Wilderness [was] being loved to death by hordes of horsemen, hikers, and campers" grew, the Deschutes and Willamette national forests "completed the preliminary draft of a management plan" that recognized the need for more intensive management to protect wilderness values threatened by overuse. "Among other things, [the draft advocated] restricting use through a permit system. If use of the wilderness continues to escalate, someday horsemen, and maybe even hikers, may need a permit to enter the Three Sisters Wilderness."[41]

Use continued to escalate over the next three decades. By the middle of the 1990s, the Three Sisters Wilderness averaged almost 60,000 visitor use days per year. About three-fifths of this visitor use occurred on the Deschutes National Forest one-third of the wilderness where visitors accessed such popular Alpine Crest Region destinations as the Green Lakes, Moraine Lake, and the South Sister via the Green Lakes

On horseback, on muleback, or afoot, Forest Service wilderness ranger Jim Leep patrolled the Three Sisters Wilderness, "caring for the land and serving people" every summer from 1993 through 2004.

Trailhead and the Devils Lake trailheads. At the end of the twentieth century, with wilderness visitation still on the increase and wilderness management budgets in steep decline, Deschutes and Willamette national forest wilderness managers faced significant challenges in implementing the Wilderness Act of 1964 in the Three Sisters Wilderness of the twenty-first century.

Suggested Reading

No tidy selection of books lends itself well to further reading on the wide-ranging subject matter briefly summarized in this chapter. The reader is referred to the bibliography to discover those references on the natural and cultural history of the Three Sisters Wilderness that will satisfy his or her needs.

---

[1] Muir, John. *My First Summer in the Sierra.* (New York: Houghton Mifflin Company, Inc., 1916) 228-229.

[2] Williams, Howel. *Volcanoes of the Three Sisters Region, Oregon Cascades.* (Berkeley: Univeristy of California Press, 1944) 37.

[3] Ibid., 53.

[4] Ibid., 43.

[5] Ellen Morris Bishop. *Hiking Oregon's Geology.* (Seattle: The Mountaineers, 1996) 106-107.

[6] Williams, 45-46.

[7] Sullivan, William L. *100 Hikes in the Central Oregon Cascades.* (Eugene: Navillus Press, 1998) 116.

[8] Williams, 55.

[9] Ibid., 58.

[10] Lynch, Ray. "Witness to Collier's Retreat." (*Eugene Register-Guard*, May 6, 1979) D1.

[11] Ibid., D2.

[12] Hodge, Edwin T. *Mount Multnomah: Ancient Ancestor of the Three Sisters.* (Eugene: University of Oregon, 1925) 137.

[13] Ibid., 146.

[14] Ibid., 137.

[15] Ibid., 141.

[16] Johnson, David M., et. al. *Atlas of Oregon Lakes.* (Corvallis: Oregon State University Press, 1985) 292.

[17] Williams, 43.

[18] Ibid.

[19] Ibid., 45.

[20] Mathews, Daniel. *Cascade-Olympic Natural History.* (Portland: Raven Editions, 1988) 17.

21 McArthur, Lewis L. *Oregon Geographic Names*. (Portland: Oregon Historical Society Press, 1992) 832.

22 Coville, Frederick V. *Forest Growth and Sheep Grazing in the Cascade Mountains of Oregon*. (Washington, D.C.: U.S. Government Printing Office, 1898) 10.

23 Merriam, Lawrence C. *Saving Wilderness in the Oregon Cascades*. (Eugene: Friends of the Three Sisters Wilderness, 1999) 2.

24 Coville, 23.

25 Ibid., 10.

26 Rakestraw, 3.

27 Coville, 10.

28 Rakestraw, 3.

29 Coville, 27.

30 Rakestraw, 39.

31 U.S. Department of Agriculture, Forest Service. "Environmental Statement for Mining Rock Mesa (Three Sisters Wilderness)." (Bend: Deschutes National Forest. November 18, 1974) 2-3.

32 Ibid., 2.

33 Rakestraw, 44.

34 *The Oregon Skyline Road*, quoted in Hatton, Raymond R. *The Sisters Country*. (Bend: Geographical Press, 1996), 69.

35 Rakestraw, 44.

36 Cleator quoted in Hatton, 70.

37 U.S. Department of Agriculture, Forest Service. *Oregon Skyline Trail Map*. (Portland: North Pacific Region, 1931) 3.

38 Merriam, 1.

39 Neal, Carl B., Forest Supervisor, Deschutes National Forest, Bend, Oregon: letter of November 19, 1934, to P.A. Thompson, Forest Supervisor, Willamette National Forest.

40 Thompson, P.A., Forest Supervisor, Willamette National Forest, Eugene, Oregon: letter of November 23, 1934, to Carl B. Neal, Forest Supervisor, Deschutes National Forest.

41 Gaston, Bob. "Over-use Endangers Wilderness Area." (*The Bulletin*, August 27, 1971)

Volunteer wilderness information specialists have served Three Sisters Wilderness visitors at the Green Lakes Trailhead Information Station, originally opened in 1992, since 1993.

Chapter Three

MANAGING THE THREE SISTERS WILDERNESS

Congress can set up and set aside the geography of hope, as it has by establishing and enlarging the National Wilderness Preservation System, but it takes something more to realize that hope. That something more is a combination of administration and stewardship—born of ethics, enlightenment, education, and experience—that adds up to the art and science of **wilderness management**. As defined by Hendee: "Wilderness management is essentially the management of human use and influences to preserve naturalness and solitude. It includes everything done to administer an area—the formulation of goals and objectives, and all policies, standards, and field actions to achieve them."[1] Management of the Three Sisters Wilderness is in the hands of the Deschutes and Willamette national forests and four of their ranger districts.

Wilderness as a Resource

As explained in Chapter One, the Wilderness Act of 1964 called for preservation and protection of wilderness "to secure for the American people ... the benefits of an enduring resource of wilderness...." A **resource**, according to Miller, "is anything obtained from the environment to meet human needs and wants."[2] To meet such needs and wants, the Wilderness Act specified that wilderness "shall be devoted to the public purposes of recreational, scenic, scientific, educational, conservation, and historic use." Thus, in the Act, **amenity resources** such as "solitude or a primitive and unconfined recreation experience" were emphasized, and **commodity resources** such as timber, minerals, and forage were either excluded or de-emphasized.

Recreation. Recreation—in the form of day hiking, overnight backpacking and camping, mountain climbing, horseback riding and packing, fishing and hunting in season, and cross-country skiing and snowshoeing—is the most familiar use of the wilderness resource. All of these activities are pursued in the Three Sisters Wilderness, where young and old alike derive physical and spiritual benefits from recreation in wild, beautiful, and challenging country. Although research indicates a nationwide decline in wilderness recreation (measured in recreation visitor days), the Three Sisters Wilderness continues to experience increases in recreational use.[3] This increase may be attrib-

utable to factors ranging from proximity to rapidly-growing population centers to exposure in regional and national media. The Three
Sisters Wilderness is the most visited wilderness in Oregon and the
twelfth most visited wilderness in the United States.[4] Closely allied to
traditional recreation use is use of wilderness for various forms of
outdoor education, human development, and therapy that enhance
both the physical and psychological wellness of individuals and society. A variety of organizations conducts such programs in the Three
Sisters Wilderness. But recreation is far from the only use of wilderness.

Scenic. Wilderness is a place of natural beauty that offers inspiration—even to those who may never enter. This beauty, in the Three
Sisters Wilderness and elsewhere, has inspired art, music, and literature.[5]

Scientific. Wilderness serves as a scientific laboratory in which
the function of ecosystems can be studied. As land managers strive to
restore diversity, resilience, productivity, beauty, and compatible
human uses, ecosystem management will require an understanding of
natural variability, large scale landscape processes, and species
evolution. Scientific research in wilderness supports these efforts.
Wilderness also provides scientists a valuable benchmark for measuring environmental changes resulting from human activities and other
causes. As David Brower said, "Wilderness holds the answers to questions we do not yet know how to ask."[6] Academic and government
scientists have long used the Three Sisters Wilderness for ecological
and other studies.

Educational. Wilderness is an outdoor classroom in which students and other visitors may learn firsthand about the natural sciences
and human relationships to the land.[7] Students from colleges, universities, and other institutions in Oregon and the rest of the United States
pursue a variety of studies in the Three Sisters Wilderness.

Conservation. Wilderness serves as a biological reserve, a store-
house for gene pools of plants, animals, and other forms of life that are
being displaced by human occupancy elsewhere. By protecting genet-
ic and species diversity, as well as ecosystem diversity, wilderness preserves life on several levels. More specifically, it protects common as
well as threatened, endangered, or sensitive animal and plant species
of current intrinsic or potential utilitarian value. For example, the
Pacific yew, which grows in the western Three Sisters Wilderness, is
the natural source of a recently discovered cancer-fighting drug.
Among the many rare and endangered species harbored in the Three

Sisters Wilderness—to name just a few—are the bald eagle, northern spotted owl, western spotted frog, and pumice grapefern. Aldo Leopold once noted that "the first law of intelligent tinkering is to save all the parts."[8] Wilderness does that, and more. Wilderness vegetation, for example, by cleaning pollutants from the atmosphere and supplying oxygen, helps maintain a healthy environment.

Historical. Wilderness is a link to America's heritage—a reminder of the nation in earlier times. It is often the site of artifacts, ranging in the Three Sisters Wilderness from Native American pictographs to early Forest Service administrative structures, which provide insights into ancient as well as more recent cultures. And it protects and preserves traditional and primitive skills—such as horse packing and use of crosscut saws—that might otherwise be lost.[9]

Wilderness also produces commodity and other economic benefits. Water—clean, fresh water for domestic, industrial, and agricultural use—is the most important of these. Congressionally designated wildernesses protect the headwaters of many regionally and nationally important rivers. Significant tributaries of the Deschutes and Willamette rivers rise in Three Sisters Wilderness watersheds. Production of mining and grazing-related commodities, allowed by the Wilderness Act as a political necessity and important within some wildernesses, has been phased out in the Three Sisters Wilderness. Some, however, view National Wilderness Preservation System units as reserves of commodities against future emergency requirements. Indeed, if under some future circumstance the commodity resources "locked up" in wilderness actually were needed, the American people through Congress could change provisions of the Wilderness Act.

Economic benefits of wilderness are related to wilderness users' willingness to pay for wilderness-related goods and services. These range from food and lodging through backpacking and mountaineering equipment to commercial outfitter-guides. Communities close to wildernesses—such as Bend, Sunriver, Sisters, McKenzie Bridge, Oakridge, and even Eugene that host Three Sisters Wilderness visitors—derive considerable economic support from that proximity. Wilderness also benefits the manufacturers of recreational equipment and the publishers of wilderness maps and guidebooks.

Wallace Stegner saw "the wilderness *idea*" as "a resource in itself." While physical wilderness "is good for us when we are young, because of the incomparable sanity it can bring briefly...into our insane lives..., it is important to us when we are old simply because it is there—important, that is, simply as an idea."[10]

The wilderness resource values mentioned so far are utilitarian values. They benefit humans directly, as either amenities or commodities. Other wilderness values are intrinsic in nature, important in and of themselves whether or not humans derive any direct use or benefit from their existence. This dichotomy of values has been explained in terms of **anthropocentric** (human-centered) and **biocentric** (nature centered) benefits. The latter, of course, are much more esoteric and difficult to discern.

Perhaps the least anthropocentric and most biocentric benefit of wilderness that people might readily grasp is the humility born of a wilderness experience properly contemplated, to respect the non-human members—the plants and animals—with which humans share the complex community of life. John Muir probably expressed this best in the 1867 journal entry cited in Chapter One. More recently, Stegner recognized wilderness as a psychic resource that shows "that we as a nation can apply some other [i.e., biocentric] criteria than commercial and exploitative considerations" and that demonstrates "our acceptance of the natural world."[11]

The wilderness resource belongs to and benefits the American people. As far as access to and use of resources are concerned, there are three categories of resources. As defined by Miller: "Any resource owned by individuals or groups of individuals is a **private property resource**," while "a **common property resource** is one to which people have virtually free and unmanaged access." Somewhere between the two are "**public property resources** ... owned jointly by all people of a country, state, or locality [and] managed for them by the government."[12] Pertinent examples of public property resources are publicly-owned lands such as the National Forest System—managed for the people by the Forest Service, and correctly referred to as "national forest lands," *not* "Forest Service lands"—and the congressionally-designated units of the National Wilderness Preservation System on national forest and other public lands. A public property resource, the Three Sisters Wilderness is managed by two ranger districts of the Deschutes National Forest and three ranger districts of the Willamette National Forest "for the American people of present and future generations."

Managing the Wilderness Resource

Wilderness must be saved twice. First, it must be saved *from* those who would develop or exploit it, then it must be saved *for* those who

Pacific Crest Trail hikers south of The Husband, Three Sisters Wilderness

would—in the oft-used phrase—"love it to death." The early leaders of the wilderness movement—people such as John Muir and, in the Forest Service, Leopold, Carhart, and Marshall, as described in Chapter One—were primarily concerned with saving wilderness from development or exploitation that would destroy it as wilderness. They assumed that designating lands as wilderness and prohibiting road construction, timber cutting, and similar activities would assure preservation of wilderness, at least for a while. But their successors soon discovered that merely to "draw a line around it and leave it alone" wouldn't save wilderness from the myriad pressures and threats of a growing and more mobile population, and the art and science of wilderness management began to evolve.

The authority of the U.S. Government to manage public lands—including National Wilderness Preservation System lands—derives from Article IV, Section 3, of the Constitution of the United States of America. This article states: "The Congress shall have Power to dispose of and make all needful Rules and Regulations respecting the Territory or other property belonging to the United States." Congress exercised that power when it passed the Wilderness Act of 1964. That Act not only defined and designated wilderness, but also directed federal public land management agencies to manage wilderness lands "for the use and enjoyment of the American people" in such a manner as to ensure "the preservation of their wilderness character." In that charge, Congress laid down the **challenge of wilderness management**. That challenge is stated simply in the first part of Hendee's definition of wilderness management as: "the management of human use and influences to preserve naturalness and solitude." Although simply stated, that definition reflects the complex **dilemma of wilderness management:** *accommodating human use while preserving wilderness quality.* Since *both* are mandated by the Wilderness Act, there is no alternative to wilderness management which, according to the second part of Hendee's definition, "includes everything done to administer [a wilderness]—the formulation of goals and objectives, and all policies, standards, and field actions to achieve them."

Wilderness management is not resource management "business as usual," as Bloedel[13] points out, and, at least in the past, has been hard for some foresters, range conservationists, and other public land managers to understand or accept. It's "not 'management' in the sense of 'doing something,' 'manipulating,' or 'improving' the resource to maximize a particular human benefit."[14] Instead, it's preservation of the wilderness resource and experience for humans to enjoy as *wilderness.* It's allowing natural processes to operate as freely as possible. "In reality," as Jerry Reese, Supervisor, Caribou and Targhee National Forest, observed, "wilderness management is often more complex than management of non-wilderness lands because of the need to maintain the delicate balance between preserving natural ecological processes and providing for human use and enjoyment of the wilderness."[15]

Although the Wilderness Act provided general guidance for National Wilderness Preservation System management, it's quite a jump from such general guidance to specific implementation within the Three Sisters Wilderness or any other wilderness. More specific guidance for management of wilderness is needed. For wilderness within the National Forest System, that guidance is provided by U.S. Department of Agriculture regulations (found in the Code of Federal Regulations, Title 36, Part 293), and by implementing Forest Service policies and directives (found in the Forest Service Manual, Title 2320) issued by the Washington, D.C., office, and supplemented by the regional offices, to the national forest supervisors and their district rangers. Wilderness managers who work for those forest supervisors and district rangers apply this guidance to develop management plans for specific wildernesses. These plans, included in specific national forest Land and Resource Management Plans (commonly called

Forest Plans) since passage of the National Forest Management Act of 1976, are implemented through detailed **Wilderness Implementation Schedules (WIS)**. While "the Forest Plan should provide the overall objectives, direction, and desired condition for each wilderness," the Washington Office specified in 1990, "the WIS should document the actions needed to manage the wilderness."[16] Thus the WIS sets forth specific actions and projects—in such realms as trail and sign management, fire management, wilderness education, etc.—that carry out the wilderness management job on the ground on a day-to-day basis. Throughout this process, wilderness managers apply "concepts, criteria, guidelines, standards, and procedures derived from the physical, biological, social, and management sciences to preserve naturalness and outstanding opportunities for solitude"[17] in the designated wilderness or wildernesses they manage. And, in so doing, they observe the following dictum:

Wilderness management should not mold nature to suit people. Rather, it should manage human use and influences so as not to alter natural process. Managers should do only what is necessary to meet wilderness objectives, and use only the minimum tools, regulation, and enforcement required to achieve those objectives.[18]

Management of the Three Sisters Wilderness is shared by the supervisors of the Deschutes National Forest in Bend and the Willamette National Forest in Eugene, and their district rangers in Bend, Sisters, McKenzie Bridge, and Oakridge. Coordination of management plans and actions by these two forests and five districts has been a continuing challenge. Suggestions of alternative approaches to this challenge have included making the Three Sisters Wilderness a single ranger district, redrawing administrative boundaries, assigning a wilderness coordinator who would supervise all on-the-ground activities for the five concerned district rangers, or assigning such a coordinator in an advisory rather than supervisory role. Since any of these alternatives could produce mixed and not necessarily improved results, the two forest supervisors and five district rangers continue to coordinate their management plans and operations.

Wilderness Management Model. The **wilderness management model** (as described in Chapter 2320 of the Forest Service Manual) illustrates the wilderness resource, as defined by the Wilderness Act, and is the basis for Forest Service wilderness management direction.

"The wilderness management model shows the relationship between the natural, undisturbed purity of a wilderness and the human

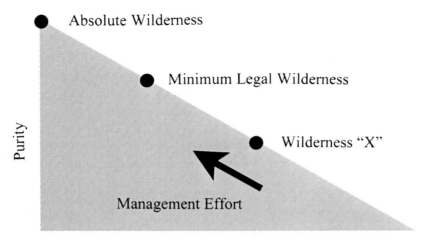

The Wilderness Management Model shows the relationship between the natural, undisturbed purity of a wilderness and the human influence that affects it. The more human influence, the lower the purity of a wilderness; the less human influence, the purer a wilderness could be.

influence that affects it. Essentially, *the more human influence, the lower the purity of a wilderness is; the less human influence, the purer a wilderness could be* [emphasis added].

"In absolute wilderness, there is no human influence preventing the area from retaining its purest natural form. It is unlikely, however, that this condition exists anywhere on earth. There are few places, if any, remaining where humans have neither set foot nor where human influences, through pollution, have not been felt. Consequently, the Wilderness Act defines wilderness at some point below absolute wilderness.

"The Act permits certain activities and contains prerogatives that also tend to lessen the opportunities to reach absolute wilderness. Mining is permitted on valid claims; access to valid occupancies and private land is provided for; and fire control, insect and disease control, grazing, and visitor use are permitted. Considered together, these modifications define legal wilderness. The objective is to manage wilderness toward attaining the highest level of purity in wilderness within legal constraints.

"Each designated wilderness is affected by a variety of human influences that vary in intensity. In one wilderness, human influence may be very limited; in another, major disturbances occur. The number and intensity of these influences causes a gap between the attainable legislative wilderness and the conditions that exist on a wilderness ("X" in the diagram). The goal of wilderness management is to identify these influences, define their causes, remedy them, and close the gap between the attainable level of purity and the level that exists on each wilderness.

"Where a choice must be made between wilderness values and visitor or any other activity, *preserving the wilderness resource is the overriding value* [emphasis added]. Economy, convenience, commercial value, and comfort are not standards of management or use of wilderness. Because uses and values vary from wilderness to wilderness, management and administration must be tailored to each. Even so, all wildernesses are part of one National Wilderness Preservation System and the management of each must be consistent with the Wilderness Act and their establishing legislation."[19]

The wilderness management model clearly reflects the wilderness management **policy of nondegradation**. This policy "recognizes that naturalness and solitude vary between individual wildernesses [and within individual wildernesses]. The objective is to prevent degradation of current naturalness and solitude in each wilderness [or portions thereof] and restore substandard settings to minimum levels, rather than [to let] all areas in the National Wilderness Preservation System deteriorate to a minimum standard."[20]

Wilderness Management Tools. Wilderness managers use a variety of tools to achieve the objectives of the wilderness management model. Some of these tools are more sophisticated than those used to maintain wilderness trails or rehabilitate wilderness landscapes. Both of the following tools—the Limits of Acceptable Change process and wilderness education—are particularly valuable to "the management of human use and influences to preserve naturalness and solitude" in wilderness and are employed in the management of the Three Sisters Wilderness.

Limits of Acceptable Change. Any human use of wilderness results in at least some resource and social **impacts** that tend to make wilderness less wild. Most use of wilderness—and virtually all use of the Three Sisters Wilderness, now virtually devoid of such non-conforming uses as mining and grazing—is recreational use, and wilderness managers focus on mitigating the effects of recreational use.

Wilderness rangers assist Three Sisters Wilderness managers in many ways, including collection of recreation impact data.

Examples of recreation-induced impacts are changes in vegetation that result from camping and trail construction and use, introduction of exotic species of plants or fish, and even transitory effects of phenomena such as crowding and aircraft overflights.

Researchers worked for decades to develop a **recreation carrying capacity** for wilderness. Such a measure may be defined as the maximum number of visitors a given wilderness or portion thereof can accommodate over time without degradation of conditions of naturalness and solitude below levels prescribed for legal wilderness. This approach suggests that the first solution to problems of resource and social impacts in wilderness should be to limit the number of recreational visitors. Among its shortcomings are a lack of recognition that different type of visitors have different levels of impact—horseback riders, for example, typically have more impact that an equal number of hikers—and that, if overused, limiting visitor numbers could reduce public support for wilderness. "The shortcomings of the carrying capacity approach resulted in recognition that 'How many are too many?' focused on the wrong question. The relevant question is 'How much change is acceptable?'"[21]

As an alternative to limiting visitor numbers, those researchers came up with the **Limits of Acceptable Change (LAC)** system that focuses on visitor impact instead of numbers of visitors. Essentially a planning tool, the LAC process requires the wilderness manager to define acceptable conditions of naturalness and solitude in various parts of a wilderness, and to prescribe actions—largely measures that reduce those visitor impacts that lead to unacceptable changes in those conditions—to maintain or achieve those conditions. Although based on the idea that many wilderness resource and social problems may be solved by reducing visitor impacts rather than limiting visitor numbers, the LAC system recognizes there are times limits may be necessary. Key LAC concepts are:

1. Some change in conditions is inevitable. Wilderness resources are not static but are constantly evolving. Natural events occur over time and space causing conditions to change. Wilderness conditions also change due to human influence. Indeed, there is no place on earth which has not been influenced in some way. Because human use is a legitimate part of Wilderness, the goal is not to eliminate all human effects but rather to determine how much change is acceptable within the intent of the Wilderness Act.

2. The focus is on human-induced change. A major goal in Wilderness management is to minimize human interference so that nature can do the "managing," thus the focus is on setting limits of change that result from human activities rather than changes that occur due to natural events (e.g., wildlife population fluctuations, fire, windthrow, avalanches). Examples of human activities are camping, trail maintenance, fire suppression, introduction of exotic species, livestock grazing, and human-induced air pollution.

3. The effects of human activities are what is important. LAC is basically a management-by-objectives approach. A fundamental concept is that management needs to focus on the desired conditions to be achieved, rather than the activities themselves. Use levels (numbers of people) can still play a role; however, use levels must be tied to the conditions managers are trying to achieve.

4. A diversity of settings is important to maintain. Diversity normally occurs within Wilderness due to differences in ease of access, topography, water sources, and proximity to towns. This results in differing levels and patterns of human use. Similarly, there are differences in the quality of habitat for various wildlife species, and thus some areas are more crucial than others. Rather than disperse human use evenly throughout the Wilderness, it is better to identify different levels of acceptable human impact. Typically, management direction is established so that some zones have very little human influence, while other zones allow for more change in conditions. This creates a spectrum of opportunities so that visitors can choose the type of wilderness experience they want and more resource protection is offered in especially sensitive areas.

5. Determining what is acceptable is value-based. LAC was intended to be an optimization process to find the best balance between conflicting desires. Standards that define acceptable conditions need to incorporate scientific knowledge regarding how human activities affect resource and experience conditions; however, what is acceptable is still based on society's values and beliefs. One assumption inherent in determining how much change is acceptable is that [one] can define the conditions that would exist without any human influence....[22]

Forest Service wilderness managers are encouraged to apply LAC concepts and the LAC process to development of wilderness management direction within a Forest Plan. As described by Stankey, "the LAC process consists of four major components: (1) the specification of acceptable and achievable resource and social conditions, defined by a series of measurable parameters; (2) analysis of the relationship between existing conditions and those judged acceptable; (3) identification of management actions necessary to achieve these conditions; and (4) a program of monitoring and evaluation of management effectiveness."[23]

In many wildernesses—and especially larger ones such as the Three Sisters Wilderness—in which the locations of trails and trailheads, destinations, and vegetation and topography combine with myriad other factors to influence use patterns, a diversity of settings and uses affects application of the LAC process. This diversity requires managers to decide where, and to what extent, varying degrees of change are appropriate and acceptable. Sometimes these decisions find expression in **management zones** which "delineate particular areas where different management prescriptions or restrictions on visitor behavior apply."[24] One approach to such zoning might include the "pristine, primitive, and portal designations, indicating decreasing degrees of naturalness and solitude." Another may identify "no-camping zones; trailless zones, where only cross-country travel and special minimum-impact camping practices are allowed; and special management zones having particular problems, high-use sites, impacted locations, or perhaps sensitive wildlife"[25] or vegetation or fragile aesthetic values. These zoning approaches reflect the concept that there is not just one desired condition for wilderness, but that a diversity of conditions and experiences may be provided in wilderness. Hendee emphasized three criteria for judging the appropriateness and utility of any wilderness zoning system:

First, remember the cardinal rule of wilderness management—*do only what is necessary.* Implement zoning restrictions only when required to protect the wilderness resource and consider the impact that the zoning would have on visitor perceptions and use.

Second, make zoning clear to users. To be effective, any zoning that requires different visitor behavior must be indicated by some reliable means such as a use permit or map.

Third, zoning' should not be used to justify nonwilderness conditions that presently exist; when such conditions exist, they should be corrected, *not* assigned to a "special management zone." Congress established wilderness as a land classification and agencies should not try to change its status through zoning.[26]

With these criteria in mind, the Deschutes and Willamette national forest managers of the Three Sisters Wilderness have applied the LAC process to develop specific management actions for a combination of three **wilderness resource spectrum zones**. Each zone has its own definition and set of management objectives that make it distinct from the other zones, and includes **special management areas** to address specific impacts.

As defined in the 1990 Deschutes National Forest land and resource management plan, these wilderness resource spectrum zones—their characteristics and wilderness experience opportunities—in the Three Sisters Wilderness are:

Semi-Primitive Zone. This area is characterized by predominantly unmodified natural environment of moderate size. Concentration of users is low, but there is often evidence of other users. The area is managed in such a way that minimum on-site controls and restrictions may be present but are subtle. Facilities are provided only for the protection of wilderness values rather than visitor comfort or convenience. Materials should be natural or natural appearing. Some relatively small transition zones may also exist adjacent to the semi-primitive zones. These areas are usually near heavily used trailheads and receive predominantly day use at a level slightly greater than that within the semi-primitive zone. The transition zone is not intended to be a permanent part of the [wilderness resource spectrum]. The long term objective is to manage these areas so that they regain the characteristics of the semi-primitive zone.

Experience Opportunity: Moderate opportunities for exploring and experiencing isolation (from the sights and sounds of people); independence; closeness to nature; tranquility and self-reliance through the application of no-trace and primitive skills in a natural environment that offers a moderate to high degree of challenge and risk.

Primitive Zone. This area is characterized by essentially unmodified natural environment. Concentration of users is low, and evidence of human use is minimal. The area is managed to be essentially free from evidence of human-induced restrictions and controls. Only essential facilities for resource protection and safety are used and are constructed of native or natural appearing materials. No facilities for comfort or convenience of the user are provided. Visitors are encouraged to disperse to desirable existing sites to minimize contacts with other groups.

Experience Opportunity: High opportunity for exploring and experiencing considerable isolation, solitude, and self-reliance through application of primitive recreation skills in an environment that offers a high degree of challenge and risk.

Pristine Zone. This area is characterized by an extensive unmodified natural environment. Natural processes and conditions have not and will not be measurably affected by the actions of users. The area is managed to be as free as possible from the influence of human activities. People are only brief visitors. Essentially no facilities are required to protect the wilderness resource. Terrain and vegetation allow extensive and challenging cross-country travel.

Experience Opportunity: Provides the most outstanding opportunity for isolation and solitude, free from evidence of past human activities and with very infrequent encounters with other users. The user has outstanding opportunities to travel cross-country utilizing a maximum degree of primitive skills, often in an environment that offers a high degree of challenge and risk.

Each of these wilderness resource spectrum zones is managed for different social objectives attained by specific standards and regulations. Encounters with other groups should be limited to no more than 10 encounters per day in the semi-primitive/transition zone, seven encounters per day in the primitive zone, and one encounter per day in the pristine zone, and these encounter standards should be met 80 percent of the time. Group size should be limited to no more than 12 people and 12 head of stock; larger groups of up to 12 people and 18 head of stock may be allowed by permit in specified areas. LAC data for such areas should demonstrate their ability to withstand the additional impacts of such groups. The 12-person group size is the maximum in pristine areas. Camps should be separated from other campsites and set back from trails, meadows, lakes, and streams at least 100 feet. No more than two other camps should be visible in the semi-primitive/transition zone, one in the primitive zone, and no other camps should be visible in the pristine zone.

Superimposed on these wilderness resource spectrum zones are special management areas in heavily-used and/or particularly-fragile parts of the Three Sisters Wilderness identified by the LAC process that found expression in regulations and restrictions imposed in 1995 to reduce visitor impacts without, but for a single exception, limiting visitor numbers. As a result, all camping in the popular Green Lakes and Moraine Lake basins and around North Matthieu, South Matthieu, Otter, and Erma Bell lakes was restricted to designated campsites. At these popular destinations, the LAC process showed, the number of campsites exceeded the number needed to meet demand and the number permitted by standards. The result was considerable damage to these sensitive areas and a degraded wilderness experience. Establishment of designated campsites followed the low-impact dictum of concentrating, rather than spreading, use in popular areas, and reduced and reversed the impact of camping on both naturalness and solitude.

Wilderness rangers obliterate informal trails to help restore parts of the Three Sisters Wilderness degraded by heavy use.

At the same time, and for similar reasons, camping setbacks were imposed in Linton Meadows and at Husband and Eileen lakes to protect fragile riparian areas. Campfires and firewood gathering are often damaging to vegetation and natural processes, particularly at frequently used sites at higher elevations. To protect heavily used and fragile areas, campfires were banned in the Green Lakes (where they have been banned since the 1970s) and Moraine Lake basins, in the Sisters Mirror Lake group and the Chambers Lakes area, and at South Matthieu, Golden, Husband, and Eileen lakes. Otherwise, campfires are prohibited within 100 feet of permanent lakes, streams, and system trails. The actual number of visitors to the heavily-used and heavily-impacted Obsidian area was limited between Memorial Day and October 31; a limited-entry permit, obtained in advance only from the McKenzie Ranger Station, is required of all who enter the area except for through-hikers on the Pacific Crest Trail. Additionally, a campfire ban and a camping setback were imposed there. Continued monitoring pursuant to the LAC process will determine if these regulations and restrictions achieve management goals, or if additional restrictions on use are required.

In particularly degraded parts of the Three Sisters Wilderness, labor-intensive rehabilitation is necessary to restore natural conditions.

Prominent among these is the peninsula at the southern end of the largest of the Green Lakes, heavily impacted by years of camping, where native vegetation has been partially restored by wilderness rangers and camping is banned. The heavily-impacted knoll on the south side of Moraine Lake, partially restored by Sierra Club volunteers and closed to camping, is another. And sections of old roads have been incorporated into the trail system, where appropriate, by encouraging plant growth in one rut, or eliminated. Preservation, of course, is preferable to rehabilitation.

Insightful wilderness managers recognize the limitations of the land classifications and impact standards that comprise some of their more esoteric management tools, and they recognize the need to develop new classifications and standards for some areas. "Proxy Falls, where the number of visitors grossly exceeds current wilderness encounter standards, doesn't fit any of the existing [wilderness resource spectrum] zones," a retired senior Forest Service wilderness manager has observed. "We need wilderness managers to figure out the proper way to manage such popular destinations and trails [as special management areas] rather than say they don't meet some artificial standard and are being 'sacrificed.'"

Regulations that govern visitor activities in the Three Sisters Wilderness, all designed to prevent unacceptable change to and protect wilderness values as required by law, are in the Code of Federal Regulations and at Appendix B. Wilderness rangers enforce these regulations. Wilderness managers, however, always prefer education to enforcement.

Wilderness Education. Wilderness education is the *sine qua non* of successful wilderness management. "Just as fire management cannot succeed without fire prevention," Gregory Hansen, a veteran Forest Service wilderness educator from the Southwestern Region, observed in1989, "wilderness management cannot succeed without impact prevention."[27] Wilderness visitors who know how to enjoy a wilderness experience and not destroy the wilderness resource are the key to "managing human use and influences to preserve natural processes." And so it is that wilderness managers, wilderness rangers, and wilderness information specialists are, or should be, wilderness teachers—at least teachers of low-impact wilderness hiking and camping ethics and skills to wilderness visitors. Former Chief of the Forest Service R. Max Peterson wrote that wilderness management is "80 to 90 percent education and information and 10 percent regulation."[28] In wilderness management, education is always preferable to enforcement.

Although the Forest Service—and, to a lesser extent, other federal wilderness management agencies—publishes and produces various wilderness education program materials and aids, wilderness education is, ultimately, a local matter. With the possible exception of the National Outdoor Leadership School's "Leave No Trace" outdoor skills and ethics program, there is no nationwide wilderness equivalent of the Cooperative Forest Fire Prevention Program that promotes Smokey Bear's wildfire prevention message to promote the wilderness impact prevention message. With national and regional guidance, each national forest and ranger district with wilderness management—and, therefore, wilderness education—responsibilities is left to develop and implement its own program. Such programs are, of course, concomitants of available talent and funds—and imagination.

A wilderness education program, if it is to be effective, is based on visitor impact reduction goals and a plan to achieve those goals within a given wilderness education environment. A recent set of goals set by a Pacific Northwest Region wilderness education study group for Forest Service wilderness managers in Oregon and Washington reads as follows:

■ To promote awareness of the unique ecological, physical, spiritual, political, and inspirational significance of the wilderness resource. To develop appreciation of this resource and to impart a spirit of stewardship with personal and social responsibility for the sustainability of the resource.
■ To demonstrate and encourage attitudes and behaviors that are appropriate to wilderness.
■ To integrate the resources of public and private partners to develop, implement, and sustain a comprehensive wilderness education program.
■ To facilitate and foster the use of wilderness education as a vital, dynamic, and invaluable component of wilderness management.
■ To establish a means of monitoring and measuring the effectiveness of wilderness education programs.

A similar set of wilderness education goals was listed by Hansen in 1989:

■ To increase visitor awareness and understanding of the Wilderness Act and the National Wilderness Preservation System.
■ To teach the visitor Leave-No-Trace, low impact camping skills.
■ To teach a general land ethic responsibility that will reach beyond the wilderness.
■ To increase the public's knowledge and understanding of the importance of non-recreational uses of wilderness.
■ To make a special effort to reach young people whose minds are receptive to new ideas.

- To create support and understanding for the wilderness natural fire program.
- To establish positive working partnerships between the managing agency and the public.
- To accomplish the above objectives without increasing the number of wilderness visitors.[29]

Wilderness managers should consider and understand objectives such as those listed above before determining the goals of a wilderness education program they would devise to meet their own circumstances and requirements. In doing so, they should identify those resources in addition to their own agency resources with which they might develop effective partnerships to implement their program. There are few national forests or ranger districts with sufficient internal resources to plan and carry out the wilderness education program that will meet their needs.

Public wilderness education may be accomplished through various vehicles and at various venues—public and private schools, youth and adult organizations and user groups, ranger station and visitor center fronts desks, etc., in town, at wilderness trailheads, and in the wilderness.

"Although it is the most challenging," wilderness visitor education in-town is the most effective because "behavioral patterns can be shaped before the visitor reaches the wilderness." These in-town educational programs, especially, "should be designed for specific age levels and specific user groups" because "generic presentations tend to be vague and uninformative."[30] They should be well planned and professionally (but not stiffly) presented by properly uniformed (in most cases) Forest Service employees or volunteers who know what they're talking about and who know how to present it effectively to the target audience. At a minimum, these programs should include an understandable explanation of the wilderness idea and its expression in the Wilderness Act and the National Wilderness Preservation System as well as the local wilderness or wildernesses. They should emphasize the benefits visitors and others derive from wilderness, the need for visitors to help keep the wilderness wild, and the low-impact practices and priority rules and regulations that apply.

Wilderness visitors who stop at ranger stations and other Forest Service offices present a special, in-town wilderness education opportunity and challenge to front desk information specialists and receptionists. These employees, who also should be uniformed agency representatives, should be sufficiently knowledgeable of the wilderness concept and local wilderness conditions to take advantage of these

Volunteer wilderness information specialists assist Three Sisters Wilderness visitors in many ways.

one-on-one educational opportunities while providing accurate answers to requests for information. It's up to wilderness managers and supervisory personnel at these stations and offices to ensure that these front desk public contact personnel are prepared for this task.

Wilderness education at wilderness trailheads usually is accomplished by trailhead signboards. At best, these tell the visitor that he or she is "about to enter a special place" designated as wilderness, provide brief information about and perhaps a map of that special place, afford wilderness permits (if required), and list wilderness regulations along with a low-impact visit message. Such signs, however, vary in quality and maintenance, and—unless attractive and authoritative in appearance as well as briefly informative—are limited in effectiveness. Cluttered, disorganized, and out-of-date trailhead signboards "turn off" wilderness visitors eager to hit the trail and are ineffective. A recently evolved set of attractive, adaptable, standardized computer-generated trailhead signs for National Wilderness Preservation System trailheads holds promise of improvement for wilderness managers whose budgets permit.

Regular trailhead staffing by wilderness information specialists, as the Deschutes National Forest has staffed the Green Lakes Trailhead entrance to the Three Sisters Wilderness since 1992, or an as-needed basis, as at a few other Three Sisters Wilderness trailheads, is a more effective wilderness education device than a sign. Such wilderness information specialists, who should be trained and uniformed volunteers, can size up a visitor or group of visitors and accomplish wilderness education goals on a one-to-one basis. Good signs, of course, can supplement this contact effort, and remain essential at most trailheads that are not staffed.

Experience shows that educational efforts of wilderness rangers in the wilderness are more effective when preceded by in-town or trailhead wilderness education experiences. Also, on-the-trail contacts by wilderness rangers have been found to be more effective in preventing impacts than in-camp visits, which occur once the visitor's camp is established, and perhaps after preventable impacts or even violations have occurred. Again, in wilderness management, education is always preferable to enforcement. If handled correctly, however, even enforcement actions can be turned into effective educational experiences. Wilderness rangers are also in a position to educate wilderness visitors by setting observable examples of low-impact hiking and camping.

The better wilderness managers supplement these traditional wilderness education approaches with less traditional approaches that take advantage of community resources. A wilderness education partnership between the Deschutes National Forest and Central Oregon Community College, both based in Bend, supports an innovative and successful sequence of two college credit wilderness courses offered at the College since 1994. This sequence affords students and other interested members of the community the opportunity to learn about the evolution and management of the National Wilderness Preservation System and to complete an internship in the Three Sisters Wilderness. The one-credit spring term course, "The Wilderness Concept and the Three Sisters Wilderness," introduces the concept of wilderness and its application to management of the Three Sisters Wilderness. This course provides a background for a follow-on wilderness internship course as well as for informed enjoyment of the wilderness. Students who complete the spring term course with a satisfactory grade and who are otherwise qualified may, with permission of the instructor, enroll in the two-credit summer term course, "Wilderness Internship." Student interns sign a Forest Service volunteer agreement and complete a minimum of 72 hours of supervised work in the Three Sisters Wilderness as wilderness information specialists.

This approach to wilderness education, which generates wilderness volunteers who serve in the Three Sisters Wilderness as well as informed wilderness visitors, is adaptable to similar situations throughout the nation where colleges and universities are located near wildernesses. Additionally, the instructor of this sequence has adapted the course content to short wilderness education programs tailored for campfire presentation and a variety of school, youth, and other organization groups throughout Central Oregon. The potential for this **Central Oregon Wilderness Education Partnership** to expand to achieve more of the Deschutes National Forest's wilderness education goals is significant.

Wilderness education isn't just for wilderness visitors and volunteers. It's also for wilderness rangers, wilderness managers, the public land managers for whom they work, and others concerned with wilderness preservation. There are wilderness education opportunities for them, too.

In addition to the wilderness management courses and programs available to students at some colleges and universities, wilderness managers and wilderness rangers already on the job—and, for that matter, anyone in the public or private sectors—may pursue a comprehensive wilderness management program without leaving the job. Originally developed at and conducted by Colorado State University in the late 1980s and early 1990s, a revised interagency **Wilderness Management Distance Education Program** has been available from The University of Montana since 1995. This program comprises four traditional correspondence courses or online courses that may be taken for college credit. These courses are:

■ Wilderness in the American Context
■ Management of the Wilderness Resource
■ Managing Recreation Resources
■ Wilderness Management Planning

These courses have been designed by representatives of the four federal wilderness management agencies, academicians, and researchers to meet a broad range of needs for government employees as well as individuals interested in wilderness preservation. This program allows Forest Service and other federal employees with limited travel and training funds a professional, cost-effective educational opportunity that will help them do a better job of caring for the wilderness resource and serving the wilderness visitor. The program is available to other students, too. Current information is available from the Center for Continuing Education, The University of Montana, Missoula, Montana 59812.

Another opportunity for wilderness rangers, wilderness managers, and other federal officials with wilderness responsibilities to enhance their wilderness management perspectives is training at the interagency **Arthur Carhart National Wilderness Training Center** in Missoula, Montana. This center was established in 1993 to "foster interagency excellence in wilderness stewardship by cultivating knowledgeable, skilled, and capable wilderness managers and by improving public understanding of wilderness philosophy, values, and processes." Staffed by an interagency team, the Carhart Center identifies challenges in wilderness management training and education, and endeavors to meet those challenges by providing consistent, professional wilderness instruction to all federal employees with wilderness responsibilities. A highlight of the Carhart Center's programs is the national interagency Advanced Line Officer Training Course, a week-long intensive workshop for senior wilderness managers and agency directors that combines wilderness experiences with classroom exercises that address wilderness management issues and concerns. The center also presents in-service training for wilderness rangers and others across the country. Deschutes and Willamette national forest personnel responsible for the Three Sisters Wilderness have attended these workshops. The Carhart Center is a sponsor of the Wilderness Management Distance Education Program offered by The University of Montana.

The closely associated **Aldo Leopold Wilderness Research Institute**, also established in 1993 in Missoula, Montana, supports the Carhart Center's training programs with research on the physical and social aspects of wilderness resource and experience management. Working together, as Carhart and Leopold did in the early years of the wilderness movement, the Carhart Center and the Leopold Institute ensure that recent developments and tested practices in wilderness management are shared throughout the ranks of federal wilderness agencies and with other organizations interested in wilderness preservation. They are prime examples of federal agencies working together to make the most of limited funding and human resources.

Wilderness Management Principles and Issues. The best possible management of any unit of the National Wilderness Preservation System results from appropriate and intelligent translation of solid, basic principles into management objectives and practices developed for and tailored to the ecological and sociological characteristics of a specific wilderness. Sixteen **principles of wilderness management,** derived from the Wilderness Act of 1964, have been tested and refined by Forest Service wilderness managers and have guided National Forest System wilderness management efforts for over 35 years. Yet, because wilderness management is such a complex pursuit, application of these principles has also raised many **wilderness management issues**.

These wilderness management principles and related issues fall into five categories: (1) overall goal of wilderness management, (2) wilderness resource management, (3) wilderness recreation management, (4) wilderness prohibitions and non-conforming uses, and (5) wilderness planning and administration. The principles within each of these categories are listed and described below. Examples of some of the myriad actions and issues associated with applying these principles to management of the Three Sisters Wilderness—many of which are contentious because they pit one set of users and values against another—are considered.

Overall Goal of Wilderness Management. One of the 16 principles addresses this goal.

Attain the Highest Level of Purity in Wilderness Character within Legal Constraints.

This is the overall goal of wilderness management—to keep the wilderness as wild and as natural as possible—and is the desired outcome of applying the wilderness management model. This involves managing for non-degradation of wilderness character by human use and, when necessary and feasible, restoring wilderness character when it has been severely damaged by human use. Examples range from measures that reduce the impacts of human use to restoring heavily impacted sites. Each wilderness is a unique ecosystem, and protective and restorative actions must be determined for each.

In the Three Sisters Wilderness, management efforts to attain the highest level of wilderness purity possible result in regulations governing camping, campfires, and other activities—especially in heavily-used areas. These regulations, in some visitors' minds, conflict with the "unconfined type of recreation" provided for in the Wilderness Act or to which they assert an unregulated right. This always will be a challenge to wilderness managers best addressed through continued wilderness education efforts.

Wilderness Resource Management. Four of the 16 principles comprise this category.

Manage Wilderness as a Distinct Resource with Inseparable Parts.

Wilderness is a unique and vital resource that produces many human benefits, not the least of which is recognition of humanity's place in nature. Wilderness managers must take care that well-intentioned management activities do not undermine the ecological processes that create and sustain the interconnected web of life in wilderness. Management decisions in favor of any one value or benefit could damage other values or benefits.

In the Three Sisters Wilderness, Deschutes and Willamette national forest Land and Resource Management Plans, as required by Forest Service policy, set standards and guidelines for integrated management of the wilderness resource. A joint WIS is developed and annually reviewed and revised by resource specialists and wilderness managers from the two supervisor's offices and five ranger districts responsible for the wilderness. This schedule identifies information requirements and collection processes that support decisions and management actions that meet those standards and guidelines on the ground. This planning process helps ensure that management decisions and actions that favor any one value or benefit—recreation, for example—don't undermine other values and benefits—natural processes, for example—to the extent feasible. A range of "real world" political, physical, and fiscal factors, of course, impinge on this management effort and modify its success. Recreation demand, for example, may influence resource protection decisions.

Manage the Use of Other Resources and Activities within Wilderness in a Manner Compatible with the Wilderness Resource.

The wilderness resource comes first. Wilderness managers should ensure that proposed management actions or activities do not harm the wilderness resource. For example, managers should not manipulate wildlife habitat to improve game populations. As another example, managers should keep recreational activities within levels that maintain the land's wilderness character, including opportunities for solitude, and retain a quality visitor experience.

In the Three Sisters Wilderness, Forest Service wilderness managers and wildlife biologists and Oregon Department of Fish and Wildlife managers and biologists are reassessing the stocking of high-country lakes—that, under natural conditions, lacked fish populations—with game fish for recreational fishing. That practice, begun in the 1920s, has compromised the wilderness's natural character and caused declines in native aquatic fauna. (While the Three Sisters Wilderness is managed by the U.S. Forest Service, management of game and fish there, under the American system of federalism, is the responsibility of the Oregon Department of Fish and Wildlife).

State fish stocking activities have improved and promoted sport fishing opportunities, but until recently have given little consideration to the riparian area impacts of fishermen or to maintenance of natural aquatic ecosystems. Moreover, wilderness solitude is disturbed by fish stocking. Aerial stocking by helicopters, albeit infrequent, may disturb visitors in the vicinity. Moreover, the increased visitation by sports fishermen occasioned by stocking may compromise a lake's remoteness, impair water quality from human and pack animal waste and trampling, and reduce native vegetation in and adjacent to aquatic-riparian ecosystems. Important to some, this may be viewed as a "non-issue" by others.

Fish stocking is a good example of a wilderness management issue for which there is no simple answer. Nothing in the Wilderness Act prohibits fish stocking, practiced in the Three Sisters Wilderness for at least forty years before it became wild by law, and fishing remains a legitimate wilderness recreation activity. Nevertheless, as in the case of other legitimate wilderness activities, fishing involves impacts that must be addressed.

Allow Natural Processes to Operate Freely.

In wilderness, natural processes govern the fortunes of plant and animal species and populations. Exotic plants and animals are not introduced. Fire, insects, and disease, play their ecological roles as much as possible. In wilderness, natural processes are not "destructive" or "good" or "bad," but *natural*. When allowing natural processes to operate freely, however, managers must protect human life and property and resources outside wilderness boundaries.

In the Three Sisters Wilderness, the goal of Deschutes and Willamette national forest fire managers is to allow fire to play its natural role. This role has been significant in the development of Three Sisters Wilderness ecosystems. Human disruption of the natural fire regime over the past 50 to 100 years has caused basic changes. Efforts to exclude fire from wilderness may have resulted in significant trends in plant and animal communities in some areas that are not consistent with the intent of the Wilderness Act. Fire suppression has allowed

Human disruption of the natural fire regime in the Three Sisters Wilderness has resulted in unnaturally high accumulations of fuels for unnaturally intense wildfires that threaten wilderness values.

unnaturally high accumulations of fuels in many places, and future fires could become unnaturally intense and result in unnatural changes to the ecosystems.

Current fire management doctrine calls for all naturally-occurring (lightning-caused) fires to be treated as wildfires and suppressed *unless* **prescribed natural fire (PNF)** direction has been approved and the fires are burning within prescribed conditions. The two forests have identified the needs to complete a PNF analysis for the Three Sisters Wilderness to assess of the risks of the use of fire to human health and safety and to lands and property outside the wilderness. Such an assessment would inform development of a PNF implementation plan to permit lightning fires to play their natural role in the wilderness in a way that minimizes risks. Such plans recognize that individual fires may disrupt recreation activities, and that it may be necessary to limit the scope and size of PNFs in special recreation zones. Unfortunately, PNF plans for the Three Sisters Wilderness face major constraints. Most significant, perhaps, is the fact that, historically, natural fires occurred in August and September when fuels were dry. Fires in these months are likely to spread beyond prescription. Regardless of potential long-term benefits, few Forest Service fire managers are willing to risk letting small fires they can control become big fires they can't. Additionally, funding constraints are likely to limit, if not entirely preclude, implementation of a PNF plan.

Development and approval of a plan to permit natural fires to play their natural role in wilderness ecosystems does not mean that human-caused wildfires would benefit wilderness. Wilderness visitors, who are more likely to start fires that disrupt recreation and damage resources than fires that benefit ecosystems, should continue to help Smokey Bear prevent wildfires.

Also, sanitation cutting of insect-infested trees—such as the lodgepole pines under attack by the mountain pine beetle in the vicinity of the Cascade Lakes Highway—stops at the Three Sisters Wilderness boundary.

Preserve Air and Water Quality

Air and water can carry pollutants that affect the health of a wilderness ecosystem. Managers should monitor and report pollution levels and implement other laws specifically designed to protect air and water quality. Internal pollution sources, such as human and domestic animal waste, should also be controlled.

In the Three Sisters Wilderness, external sources of pollution are relatively minimal because of remoteness from urban and industrial areas. To control internal sources of pollution, which have made it risky to drink water from streams and lakes without purifying it first, wilderness managers, rangers, and information specialists encourage visitors to practice "Leave No Trace" techniques of properly disposing of waste that cannot be packed out. These include: (1) depositing human waste in "cat holes" dug six to eight inches deep and at least 200 feet from water, camp, or trails; (2) using toilet paper or wipes sparingly, and packing them out; and (3) bathing and washing cooking utensils or clothing at least 200 feet from streams or lakes with small amounts of biodegradable soap. These and other such techniques are at Appendix C. Dog and livestock feces present a particularly challenging pollution and public health problem for wilderness managers. Additionally, regulations prohibit "building, attending, maintaining, or using a campfire within a 100-foot slope distance of any permanent water source," and "hitching, tethering, picketing, or securing any pack or saddle stock within a 200-foot slope distance of any permanent water source." These measures help preserve water quality by preventing erosion and pollution.

Wilderness Recreation Management. Four of the 16 principles comprise this category.

Produce Human Values and Benefits while Preserving Wilderness Character.

The Wilderness Act recognizes that wilderness is for people to visit or otherwise use and enjoy *as wilderness.* But it also emphasizes the importance of wilderness as a natural store of biological diversity and scientific values. Wilderness managers should not be so protective of the ecosystem that they unnecessarily limit opportunities for people to enjoy wilderness. Preservation of natural wilderness ecosystems produces long-term benefits for people.

In the Three Sisters Wilderness, wilderness managers always walk this decision-making tightrope inherent in the wilderness management dilemma of accommodating human use while preserving wilderness quality. Virtually every management decision involves balancing anthropocentric and biocentric values. Given the range of visitor perceptions of wilderness and of their rights and responsibilities *vis-à-vis* wilderness, this is a challenge that wilderness managers and their representatives in the field must meet constantly and creatively through a balanced wilderness education program. A realization that managing this dilemma "goes with the territory" helps.

Preserve Outstanding Opportunities for Solitude and Primitive and Unconfined Recreation Experiences

One of the most important benefits of wilderness to humans is the opportunity to enjoy solitude in an outdoor setting free of most of the controls of modern society, "to get away from it all." Wilderness managers should leave visitors alone, and plan for the least amount of contact with or control over visitors. Visitors should be allowed to freely camp in a primitive manner. Campsite convenience structures should not be furnished. But visitor use levels should not be allowed to reach the point at which the individual visitor's solitude is destroyed or evidence of humans dominates. While visitors should be allowed freedom from excessive management regulations, some rules are the only effective means of preventing damage to the wilderness experience and the wilderness resource.

In the Three Sisters Wilderness, wilderness information specialists at trailheads and wilderness rangers in the wilderness strive to preserve *both* the wilderness experience and the wilderness resource by minimizing the number and maximizing the effectiveness of visitor

Wilderness solitude standards are exceeded regularly on the popular South Sister summit as well as on the more popular Three Sisters Wilderness trails.

contacts. The primary purpose of such contacts is informing and educating visitors about the few regulations and practices necessary to keep the wilderness wild.

Managing access to ensure the "outstanding opportunities for solitude" called for in the Wilderness Act is an emerging and thorny issue for Deschutes and Willamette national forest wilderness managers. This is especially true in the more crowded corridors of the Three Sisters Wilderness: the trails leading from Cascade Lakes Highway trailheads to the Green Lakes, Moraine Lake, and the South Sister summit, and the trails leading from Oregon Highway 242 trailheads to the Obsidian area and Proxy Falls. At issue is interpretation of the sentence in the Act which states that wilderness "has outstanding opportunities for solitude or a primitive and unconfined type of recreation" on which this wilderness management principle is based. As Nelson pointed out, advocates of solitude, on the one hand, claim that the Act requires the Forest Service "to manage every acre to protect the opportunity for solitude" even if that means enforcing solitude standards with a "solitude based permit system." Advocates of unrestricted access, on the other hand, argue that "solitude is not guaranteed by the Wilderness Act" and that "when people are turned away, wilderness loses potential advocates. Some...suggest that heavily used trails

should be 'sacrificed' to crowds so other trails remain [less traveled]."
They also point out that "solitude is subjective" and cite a recent
Alpine Lakes Wilderness study that "found that half the visitors [on a
particular heavily used wilderness trail] said meeting other hikers
didn't detract from their experience."[31]

Any effort to limit access to additional Three Sisters Wilderness
trails to attain solitude should be informed by objections voiced by
some wilderness users to the Mt. Hood National Forest's late 1990s
plans to implement "draconian" access limits to popular trails in the
Mt. Hood Wilderness in pursuit of an "abstract concept." As *The
Bulletin* in Bend editorialized:

> People...are pretty flexible and intelligent creatures. ... a solitude seeker ... has
> the option of doing so on an off-peak weekend—or taking a vacation day and doing
> it during the week.
>
> By ignoring this simple fact and throwing up a turnstile at every popular trail-
> head, the Forest Service runs the very real risk of alienating the legions of people who
> would be turned aside. By and large, people who use forest trails develop a sense of
> ownership. They take an interest in keeping them maintained and funded.
>
> People who are turned aside from public land—especially public land hard by a
> large city—so that a few selected others can stroll by their lonesome doesn't promote
> ownership. It promotes resentment and anger.
>
> If the Forest Service wants to build public support, it ought to scrap the patron-
> izing practice of shielding people from each other and treat them instead as intelli-
> gent creatures capable of deciding where to hike, and when.[32]

Given funding cuts, the issues of solitude-based permit systems and
access limits that would require more staff both in the office and in the
wilderness may be left to resolve themselves. Other actions, such as
reconstructing the popular Green Lakes Trailhead parking area to
reduce its capacity and developing a five-mile "one-way" loop trail
opportunity as an alternative to the nine-mile round trip to the Green
Lakes could "reduce use impacts to the Green Lakes area" and "reduce
social impacts."[33]

Control and Reduce the Adverse Physical and Social Impacts of Human Use in Wilderness through Education and Minimum Regulation.

When human use must be controlled to preserve the wilderness
experience and prevent wilderness resource damage, this is best done
in an order of increasing control: (1) education in proper wilderness
camping and travel techniques; (2) indirect control methods, such as
dispersion of use; and (3) the minimum regulation of use necessary to

meet management objectives. In cases of overuse, specific steps should be taken to reduce physical and social impacts. Tighter temporary or long-term controls through a permit or quota system may be necessary. Restoration of damaged sites through natural or artificial means may be justified. Education is always preferable to enforcement.

In the Three Sisters Wilderness, information about low-impact wilderness camping and travel techniques and regulations based on those techniques is available at all trailheads and from wilderness information specialists and wilderness rangers who also encourage visitors to enjoy the less-frequented parts of the wilderness. The preferred wilderness education practice of reaching visitors with appropriate messages *before* they arrive at wilderness trailheads is limited to the effectiveness of a few national programs. The Leave No Trace program of the National Outdoor Leadership School is the most extensive of these. User group training provided by Deschutes and Willamette national forest wilderness employees and volunteers compliment and supplement national efforts.

In areas of the Three Sisters Wilderness that are overused, steps to reduce visitor impacts include limited entry permits, such as those required since 1995 to visit the popular Obsidian area, and designated campsites and campfire bans. Designated campsites have been established in high-use areas where the numbers of actual campsites exceed the number necessary to meet both demand and solitude standards. Campfire bans have been imposed in high use and high elevation areas where firewood gathering would damage vegetation.

Although most Three Sisters Wilderness visitors understand and support such measures, a few object to anything they perceive as government infringements on their rights, freedoms, and the "primitive and unconfined recreation experience" mentioned in the Wilderness Act. A study conducted by Oregon State University for the Deschutes National Forest in 1997 "suggests that a proposal to limit use will be met with opposition.... Only 28 percent of the [visitors surveyed at the Green Lakes Trailhead] said forest officials should reduce or cap use, while 72 percent favored no reduction or cap."[34]

As a rule, Three Sisters Wilderness managers prefer education that limits visitor impacts to regulation that limits visitor numbers. Yet, in the early years of the twenty-first century, visitor number limits, in place in the Obsidian area since 1995, are again being considered for such popular areas as the Green Lakes, Moraine Lake, and South Sister.

Favor Wilderness Dependent Activities.

Wilderness is a scarce resource, and many recreational or other activities taking place in wilderness can be enjoyed elsewhere. Pursuits that require a wilderness environment should receive priority where there are competing demands for human use. Wilderness managers should not wait for severe conflicts between activities to occur before shifting non-dependent activities outside of the wilderness.

In the Three Sisters Wilderness, jogging and high school cross-country team practice, both well-established non-dependent activities, sometimes conflict with foot and horseback travel by visitors whose *primary* objective is a wilderness experience rather than physical conditioning or preparation for athletic competition. Conflicts between joggers and horseback riders over trail right-of-way are often as acrimonious as they are avoidable; a little common sense and civility could go a long way toward preventing these "run-ins." Also among non-dependent and inappropriate activities are such "radical" pursuits as white water kayaking on wilderness creeks that invades solitude and may damage fragile riparian areas. Exercising dogs is another non-dependent activity considered inappropriate, harmful, and even dangerous by many. There are, however, no regulations that either govern or prohibit these and many other non-dependent activities.

Wilderness Prohibitions and Non-Conforming Uses.
Two of the 16 principles comprise this category.

Exclude the Sight, Sound, and Other Tangible Evidence of Motorized Equipment or Mechanical Transport Wherever Possible.

One of the most important directions in the Wilderness Act is to ban the use of motorized equipment and mechanical transport within wilderness. The Act allows managers to approve their use in emergencies or if they are necessary minimum tools for a wilderness management task. Previously established aircraft and motorboat use and motorized access to private inholdings [and to certain permitted activities such as grazing and mining] may be permitted to continue. (The Alaska National Interest Lands Conservation Act of 1980 provides for general public motorized travel in the wildernesses it established.) Therefore, the management goal is to exclude the evidence of these activities wherever possible. Managers must take the lead demonstrating that management tasks can be performed well by primitive or traditional non-motorized methods.

A mounted wilderness ranger in the Three Sisters Wilderness doubles as a packer, transporting material and equipment as he patrols trails and serves visitors.

In the Three Sisters Wilderness, Forest Service wilderness personnel travel on foot or horseback. They transport equipment and materials in backpacks or on pack stock, and use hand tools exclusively (much to the chagrin of some wilderness visitors who think wilderness trails should be "logged out" more quickly with chain saws) in performing their duties. All forms of motorized equipment—except Air Life of Oregon helicopters in genuine emergencies, as approved by the appropriate forest supervisor, and helicopters, chain saws, and portable pumps used in fire fighting, which may be authorized on a case-by-case basis—are banned from the wilderness. "Possessing or using bicycles, wagons, carts, or wheelbarrows (except wheelchairs)" in the wilderness—except when Deschutes and Lane county sherifff's office search and rescue personnel employ non-motorized, wheeled litters to evacuate accident victims—is prohibited.

Wilderness information specialists at staffed trailheads provide mountain bikers with map folders describing alternative mountain biking opportunities outside the wilderness, and loan special backpacks for carrying infants and small children to visitors who arrive at those trailheads with wheeled strollers.

Mountain bikers and riders of motorized off-highway vehicles, and—during the winter—snowmobile operators, either ignorant of or intentionally ignoring posted regulations and boundaries, occasionally violate the Three Sisters Wilderness, and adversely impact the wilderness experiences of others and damage the wilderness resource. Wilderness rangers and other law enforcement officers warn or cite such violators as their infractions warrant. Clearly posting more of the wilderness boundary may help reduce the number of these incidents that are honest mistakes.

Remove Existing Structures and Terminate Uses and Activities Not Essential to Wilderness Management or Not Provided for by Law.

Wilderness managers should lead the way in demonstrating that not all existing structures are necessary for wilderness management and use. Administrative cabins, lookouts, trail shelters, radio towers, weather stations, and the like have a huge impact on one of the more important characteristics of wilderness—that it is a place not occupied or modified by humans.

In the Three Sisters Wilderness, Horse Lake Guard Station was removed in 1972, possibly because the stringent purity standard the Forest Service applied to wilderness *at the time* reflected a belief that "the presence of historical structures and other cultural resources [was] incompatible with wilderness"[35] and what Throop called "an imperfect understanding of the wilderness resource and the objectives of wilderness management."[36] In applying this principle, wilderness managers must not interpret—or misinterpret—the intent of the Wilderness Act in a way that would cause them to violate the National Historic Preservation Act of 1966 passed "to ensure that federally funded or permitted undertakings do not inadvertently destroy cultural resources important to our [national] heritage."[37] Among misconceptions about management of heritage resources in wilderness is the view that they "represent those very human works that are generally precluded by the Wilderness Act. The Wilderness Act, however, specifically recognized the preservation of historical values as a *purpose* of wilderness. Section 2 (c) of the Act defines wilderness as an area that '*generally* appears to have been affected *primarily* by the forces of nature, with the imprint of man *substantially* unnoticeable' (emphasis added). Nowhere does the Act state that an area must be pristine with no evidence of human activity."[38] Forest Service policy did "not preclude retention of National Register [of Historic Places] eligible buildings in wilderness, but in practice management

Muskrat Lake Cabin, Three Sisters Wilderness

direction [encouraged] abandonment."[39] Based on the policy that "Regional Foresters may approve stabilization or restoration of such structures *if their continued existence is essential to cultural resource management*" (emphasis added), the Pacific Northwest Region developed "a process for determining which buildings in wilderness meet that essential standard."[40] The old Olallie and Rebel Rock fire lookouts, three old Oregon Skyline Trail shelters at James Creek, Mink Lake, and Cliff Lake, and the 1934 log cabin at Muskrat Lake have been or will be evaluated for their heritage resource value under this standard, and may or may not remain. Smashed by falling trees in 1997, the Olallie Guard Station is no longer an issue. Meanwhile, old roads such as the U.S. Pumice Company's road across the Wickiup Plain are being narrowed and integrated into the trail system, or returned to a natural state.

Wilderness Planning and Administration. Five principles comprise this catogory.

Accomplish Necessary Wilderness Work with the "Minimum Tool."
Wilderness managers should scrutinize each and every planned management action to determine that it is necessary, then plan to accomplish it with the *minimum tool* required. The **minimum tool** has

Directional and regulatory signs in the Three Sisters Wilderness are used only where absolutely necessary.

the least discernible impact on the land and is the least manipulative or restrictive means of achieving a management objective. For example, trailhead information boards that explain wilderness regulations are less restrictive and less invasive than posting warning signs or law enforcement staff in the wilderness. Likewise, hand tools create less lasting impacts than motorized equipment, and managers should train wilderness workers in the use and maintenance of traditional hand tools and primitive travel methods. Wilderness manager leadership in the minimum tool approach sets a good example for wilderness visitors.

In the Three Sisters Wilderness, the minimum tool concept guides management and maintenance work. Trailhead information programs are emphasized, and directional and regulatory signing as well as information and enforcement staffing inside the wilderness is minimized. All work is accomplished with hand tools such as two-person crosscut saws that are quieter than chainsaws, and the lowest-impact primitive travel method usually is used.

Establish Specific Management Objectives, with Public Involvement, in a Management Plan.

Wilderness managers and wilderness users, working together to apply these principles derived from the Wilderness Act, should define standards of acceptable conditions and management practices for each wilderness. These should be documented in a management plan. It is essential that wilderness visitors and other users understand the purpose of wilderness and support management decisions.

In the Three Sisters Wilderness, such standards and practices are defined in Deschutes and Willamette national forest Land and Resource Management Plans. These plans are translated into action by Wilderness Implementation Schedules developed and annually reviewed and revised by wilderness managers and resource specialists from the two forest supervisors' offices and five ranger districts responsible for the wilderness. This planning and scheduling is informed by the LAC process.

These plans and schedules are developed in consultation with a wide range of interested publics. In the fall of 1992, for example, a 26-member citizens' focus group representing the full range of wilderness users assisted these managers in evaluating wilderness use data and recommending actions to reduce the adverse effects of recreation use. The intent was to focus on recreation use situations that exceeded Forest Plan standards, and recommend specific actions to the two forest supervisors responsible for the final decisions. The focus group supported some measures for wilderness-wide use, others for use in those parts of the wilderness where encounter and campsite conditions exceeded standards.

For the entire wilderness, the focus group recommended education of wilderness visitors before they arrive in the wilderness, use of qualified volunteers in this effort, and continued monitoring of campsite conditions and encounter frequencies to determine use trends and assess effectiveness of management actions.

For those parts of the wilderness in which use exceeds standards, the focus group recommended that wilderness managers:

■ limit the number of day and/or overnight visitors by setting quotas;
■ restrict or prohibit campfires, especially in alpine and sub-alpine areas where vegetation recovery is slow;
■ designate campsites and/or reduce the size of campsites through rehabilitation;
■ designate sites for stock watering, highlines, and grazing in areas where stock use has heavily impacted campsites, lakes, and meadows; and
■ reduce the effects of trails on campsite conditions, and the number of encounters a visitor has by designating one-way loops, eliminating trails in riparian areas, and reducing the size or location of trailheads.

Most of these focus group recommendations are reflected in current Three Sisters Wilderness regulations or have been incorporated into management plans or actions.

Harmonize Wilderness and Adjacent Land Management Activities.

Wilderness does not exist in a vacuum. Managers should plan activities on both sides of wilderness boundaries in a manner that recognizes differing land management goals. For example, constructing a large campground or a large parking lot at a wilderness trailhead can lead to overuse. Or, severe insect outbreaks within a wilderness may cause unacceptable damage to valuable resources outside the wilderness if not controlled.

In the case of the Three Sisters Wilderness, the Cascade Lakes watershed analysis conducted by the Deschutes National Forest supports management decisions affecting the interacting processes in the eastern interface of wilderness and non-wilderness lands. Additionally, the decision to reconstruct the Green Lakes Trailhead parking lot as a smaller wilderness access facility addressed a significant case of overuse in the wilderness.

Manage Wilderness with Interdisciplinary Scientific Skills.

Because of the complex relationships involved, wilderness managers need the skills of physical, biological, and social scientists to preserve wilderness. An interdisciplinary team must focus on preserving wilderness as a resource.

In the Three Sisters Wilderness, interdisciplinary teams of wilderness managers and resource specialists accomplish wilderness management planning and operations.

Manage Special Exceptions Provided for by Wilderness Legislation with Minimum Impact on the Wilderness Resource.

The Wilderness Act protected the interests of private landowners and established exceptions for activities that do not normally conform to the wilderness concept—such as valid mining claims and livestock grazing—that existed before the law was passed. Subsequent wilderness legislation also provided for special management exceptions. All exceptions should be managed in a manner that adheres to the Act's basic management direction and creates the least impact on the wilderness resource.

In the Three Sisters Wilderness, the wilderness resource is relatively unaffected by such non-conforming exceptions as mining—there are no valid claims, and no new ones may be filed—and grazing, and such exceptions are not a major management concern. The 1983 buyout of the U.S. Pumice Company's valid claim to mine Rock Mesa and the phasing out of livestock grazing represent management decisions that eliminated special exceptions to the benefit of the wilderness resource.

These principles are the basic management direction for national forest wildernesses. Guided by these principles, wilderness managers develop specific management practices that "fit" the ecological and social characteristics of each wilderness. Forest Service wilderness directives provide further specific advice, but no directive system can answer all the questions that arise in managing wilderness. A wilderness manager who is well grounded in these principles will make good wilderness management decisions.

Wilderness Management Success. A wilderness manager may assess success by asking if the wilderness management effort:

■ ensures that natural processes operate freely so that the land's primeval character and influence are retained;
■ ensures that the wilderness is not occupied or modified so that natural conditions are dominant and the imprint of humans is substantially noticeable;
■ ensures that there are opportunities for solitude or a primitive and unconfined type of recreation;
■ ensures that spirituality and the elements of surprise, discovery, and self reliance are retained;
■ ensures support of the wilderness resource in its entirety;
■ recognizes the unique characteristics of the particular wilderness;
■ complies with Congress's intent for managing the special provisions within wilderness; and
■ ensures that future generations will be able to enjoy the benefits of an enduring resource of wilderness.[41]

Wilderness Managers, Wilderness Rangers, and Wilderness Information Specialists

Wilderness Managers. Wilderness managers are employed by the Forest Service and the three other federal wilderness-managing agencies to carry out the stewardship mandate of the Wilderness Act of 1964 on the National Wilderness Preservation System units, unit, or sub-unit in their charge. Some, educated and experienced in other aspects of natural resource management, have come to wilderness in the middles of their careers and have had to learn about the wilderness concept and about how and why wilderness is different from other public lands. More, trained in wildland recreation management and even wilderness management, entered the federal service to be wilderness managers, have applied the wilderness concept as they have addressed wilderness management issues throughout their careers, and have been wilderness users throughout their lives. Whatever their backgrounds, unless and until wilderness managers grasp the special nature of wilderness, many of the recommended and mandated wilderness management practices they follow may seem inadequate, untimely, or even incorrect when compared with the practices of public land managers outside of wilderness. Perhaps more important is the fact that wilderness management manuals and handbooks cannot cover every possible condition that may be encountered or practice that may be warranted, and wilderness managers must be able to come up with their own appropriate, consistent, and timely solutions in the absence of written direction. Every wilderness is unique, and there is no one recipe for success.

The successful wilderness manager's solutions are informed by values that are, in many ways, wider than those usually employed to manage natural resources on public lands. These values make wilderness and wilderness managers different. Without a thorough understanding of this difference—of the unique benefits and values held only by wilderness, the wilderness manager may have a hard time convincing himself or herself, other resource managers, or the public that his or her actions are correct. Wilderness managers need a special vision that both recognizes and transcends the recreational value of wilderness, for there's much more to wilderness than recreation.

Along with wilderness values, the wilderness manager's work benefits from a wilderness ethic. This ethic provides a moral foundation that helps a manager make the right decisions. As Leopold wrote: "A thing is right when it tends to preserve the integrity, stability, and beauty of the community, ...the soil, waters fauna, and flora, as well as people. A thing is wrong when its tends otherwise."[42]

Armed with wilderness values, a wilderness ethic, education, experience, an understanding of the Forest Service as an organization and how to work within it, and common sense, a wilderness manager is ready to tackle that job with the built-in dilemma of accommodating human use while preserving wilderness character. A successful wilderness manager has to be a bureaucrat in the positive sense of the term. It is the wilderness manager who develops the wilderness direction that becomes part of the Forest Plan. To get his or her ideas incorporated into the plan, he or she must understand the planning process and win the support of other resource managers. To implement his or her ideas, he or she must understand the budgetary process and

Wilderness rangers work with people to help keep the wilderness wild and promote good wilderness experiences.

compete successfully for scarce funds. And there's more. Ultimately, success at that job depends on how well that manager is able to recruit and organize people—employees and, increasingly important in an era of declining budgets, volunteers—needed to translate wilderness management plans into action. It is through people—properly motivated, organized, and trained wilderness rangers, wilderness educators, and wilderness information specialists, as well as resource specialist colleagues—that the wilderness manager accomplishes his jobs of informing and educating visitors and managing the resource.

Wilderness Rangers. Wilderness rangers, under the supervision of wilderness managers, do the wilderness management job "on the ground" to prevent wilderness resource degradation and enhance wilderness visitor experiences. Wilderness rangers, on foot and on horseback, patrol the wilderness—as the Forest Service motto puts it—"caring for the land and serving people." In the Three Sisters Wilderness, where most wilderness rangers travel on foot as do most wilderness visitors, a few mounted rangers sometimes double as packers and relate especially well to wilderness visitors on horseback.

While these rangers—in the Three Sisters Wilderness, both employees and volunteers—spend much of their time maintaining wilderness facilities (trails and signs), rehabilitating wilderness campsites and landscapes, and monitoring use conditions and gathering management information, their most important job is visitor information and education. Wilderness rangers work with people to help keep the wilderness wild. Since wilderness visitors represent a cross-section of American society as well as foreigners, this requires the ability to relate to a wide variety of people in a manner that elicits voluntary and willing compliance with wilderness regulations and practice of low-impact techniques. Of course, wilderness rangers also provide emergency fire fighting and search and rescue services when necessary.

It takes more than love of the wilderness, backpacking skills, and physical stamina to succeed as a wilderness ranger. A strong commitment to public service, an intimate knowledge of the wilderness concept and its realization in the National Wilderness Preservation System, a working knowledge of the wilderness in which employed, and both a willingness to represent an agency and an idea and a knack for effective public contact are essential. So is a love of people. Anyone who takes up wilderness work to get away from people takes up the wrong line of work. Wilderness management is people management, and wilderness rangers are on the leading edge of that effort. Since wilderness rangers are in the public eye, and often the only representatives of the Forest Service that wilderness visitors meet, they must both be and be seen by the public as competent and dedicated public servants. In addition to being clean, well groomed, and properly uniformed, they must articulate wilderness knowledge and exemplify wilderness behavior in all they say and do.

As inviting as the job of wilderness ranger may sound, the Forest Service often has difficulty recruiting capable and qualified people who are available and willing to serve in these rigorous, three-month, temporary positions for low pay. All too often the job falls to unqualified employees or even unsupervised volunteers who, in their dealings with wilderness visitors, may do the wilderness concept and the wilderness management effort more harm than good. At the extreme ends of the spectrum, neither the "laid-back hippie" type nor the "badge-heavy cop" type is appropriate for this important public service.

As the established leader in federal wilderness management, the Forest Service should be able to emphasize selective recruiting and rigorous training of an elite corps of full-time wilderness specialists possessed of the education, ethics, enthusiasm, and endurance equal to the challenge of wilderness ranger service. Such full-time specialists

Volunteer wilderness information specialists pursue "a friendly face and a helping hand" approach to serving wilderness visitors.

could spend the winters accomplishing wilderness management planning and wilderness education missions, and the entire field season in the wilderness as wilderness rangers. Similarly selected and qualified seasonal employee and volunteer wilderness rangers, who would be trained for and return to the job year after year, would be supervised by and supplement these full-time professionals. Annual wilderness ranger academies should be established at which both career and part-time personnel would train, and at which the unfit would be weeded out. All this would be expensive, but the National Wilderness Preservation System and the American public deserve nothing less than the best in this vital job. Congress, however, has been unwilling to appropriate sufficient funds to develop and support such a corps.

Wilderness Information Specialists. As their wilderness management budgets and staffing have been cut during the late 1990s and early 2000s, the Deschutes and Willamette national forests increasingly have turned to volunteers to supplement their dwindling wilderness ranger forces and serve their increasing visitor populations. Perhaps the most ambitious volunteer program in the Three Sisters Wilderness is the wilderness information specialist program pioneered by the Bend Ranger District (now the Bend-Fort Rock Ranger District) in 1993. That year, volunteers who know the Three Sisters Wilderness and are otherwise qualified were first recruited and trained to staff the Green Lakes Trailhead Information Station at the most-used entrance to the wilderness and to serve at other trailheads as uniformed Forest Service representatives. They've been on the job every summer since, and have kept the Green Lakes Trailhead station open every day between July 1 and Labor Day and performed other trailhead and wilderness duties.

Qualified persons at least 18 years of age who will commit to at least eight days of service during the summer wilderness visitor season may apply for service as wilderness information specialists. From 10 to 20 volunteers from all walks of life—to whom the Forest Service provides pre-season and on-the-job training, uniforms, equipment, and supervision—qualify and serve as wilderness information specialists each year. While some serve only one summer, others return summer after summer. All must present "a friendly face and a helping hand" to the public and meet a high standard of service.

Working alone or in pairs, these wilderness information specialists assist wilderness users and other national forest visitors by providing information about wilderness travel and regulations—or anything else a visitor may wish to know—and helping with the wilderness permit and, since 1997, user fee systems. They squeeze in low-impact hiking and camping messages whenever they can. They also gather visitor statistics, maintain trailhead facilities, and assist in emergencies. Some patrol wilderness trails and perform other duties. Statistics show they contact between 6,000 and 8,000 visitors just at the Green Lakes Trailhead each summer. These volunteers, while not federal employees, receive legal protection as well as insurance for work-related injuries and, if funds are available, reimbursement for certain expenses.

Funding Wilderness Management

Wilderness management, especially management of wilderness recreation, costs money. Yet, during the latter 1990s, as Three Sisters Wilderness visitation steadily increased, Deschutes and Willamette national forest wilderness management budgets steadily decreased. After peaking in 1995, these budgets had been cut severely by the end of the decade. Indeed, most such Forest Service budgets have been slashed. By the late 1990s, funding for the Three Sisters Wilderness—and for many if not most other National Wilderness Preservation System units—had dropped to the point that trail patrols and maintenance, as well as other management activities, had been severely curtailed. A backlog of trail maintenance and other wilderness projects had built up, and more of this work had fallen to volunteers to accomplish.

In 1996, as an alternative to authorizing adequate appropriations, Congress authorized the **Recreation Fee Demonstration Program** for three years. As outlined by the Omnibus Consolidated Recissions and Appropriations Act of 1996, this program allowed the Forest Service and other federal wilderness management agencies to explore new ways to generate revenue to improve recreation services and protect recreation resources. In effect, Congress told the Forest Service that it would not appropriate the funds needed to carry out the mandate of the Wilderness Act of 1964, but that it would authorize the Forest Service to raise its own funds to carry out that mission by charging user fees. These fees, essentially ordered by Congress, soon became a major issue in outdoor recreation. Across the nation, while most visitors who traveled long distances to visit wildernesses didn't seem to mind paying these fees and often posted high compliance rates, many local residents tended to resent and resist paying fees.

In its Pacific Northwest Region, the Forest Service developed the Trail Park Project, as part of the Recreation Fee Demonstration Program, to generate funds for trail and trailhead facility maintenance. Visitors who used about 900 trailheads on eight national forests in Oregon and Washington during 1997 purchased $3.00 day passes or $25.00 annual passes—not to use the trails *per se*, but to park vehicles at trailheads—that were displayed on their vehicles' windshields. Eighty percent of the funds generated by this new user fee were to be retained by and used by the national forests where they were collected. Both the Deschutes and Willamette national forests participated in this project in 1997, and Trail Park passes were required at most Three Sisters Wilderness trailheads. Five additional national forests in the region joined the Trail Park Project in 1998, while the remaining six opted not to participate.

This new user fee, charged for parking at trailheads that had been "free" for generations, met with mixed responses from Three Sisters Wilderness users that ranged from enthusiastic support to protest and boycott. At the latter extreme, some disputed the stated objectives of the Trail Park Project and saw it, instead, as part of a conspiracy between big business and the federal government to exploit recreation on the public lands for private profit. Some opponents promoted the idea that "big business has worked with a number of key lawmakers to slash recreation spending to make agencies dependent on private sources of financing" to the degree that "people with the pro-development, pro-profit motivation will become the eventual managers of our public lands."[43] Others, including some Forest Service wilderness managers, dismissed such conspiracy theories but expressed concern "that some forest managers will begin making decisions based on revenue projections rather than on long-term resource management"[44] criteria, and that this could prove detrimental to the wilderness resource and the wilderness experience. Still others objected to user fees that they believed charged taxpayers twice for the same service or prevented the poor from accessing public recreation. Media coverage tended to focus on negative responses to the user fee project.

Many wilderness visitors, and most of those entering the Three Sisters Wilderness via the Green Lakes Trailhead, were willing—and some even eager—to purchase Trail Park passes. This was especially the case because volunteer Forest Service wilderness information specialists who staff the Green Lakes Trailhead Information Station explained the reason for the new user fee and made the passes readily available. At that trailhead, compliance with the user fee system ranged from 80 to 90 percent compared with about 55 percent elsewhere. By the beginning of the 1998 season, most wilderness visitors knew about the user fee requirement.

During the next several years, as the user fee controversy continued and as Congress passed three two-year extensions of the Recreation Fee Demonstration Program, the program's emphasis—as far as wilderness trails are concerned—shifted from maintaining trails accessed via trailheads as the amenity supported by fees to the facilities at trailheads (and other recreation sites). Reflecting this change, the Trail Park Pass became the Northwest Forest Pass in 2000. As time passed, the search for simplicity and nationwide consistency reflected in almost annual changes to the user fee and pass system. Finally, in late November 2004, Congress included the proposed Federal Lands Recreation Enhancement Act that would authorize federal recreation fees for 10 years as a rider on the Omnibus Appropriations Bill that President George W. Bush signed into law in early December 2004. Effectively, this Act made the recreation fee system permanent; it is no longer a demonstration, and wilderness management is likely to continue to depend on user fees.

The challenge to the Forest Service and its wilderness managers in the user-fee era—an era that will last as long as the American public permits Congress to cut recreation budgets in favor of user fees—is to make compliance as convenient and comprehensible as possible. And, of course, the public has to see that its money is used wisely in the management of wilderness and other national forest recreation resources. "Our critical test is our accountability," then-Chief of the Forest Service Mike Dombeck observed in June 1977 when the Recreation Fee Demonstration Program first was implemented. "We have to put that money back into the areas where it came from. At the same time, Dombeck emphasized that user fees are "not a substitute for appropriations" from Congress.

Citizen Involvement in Wilderness Preservation and Management

When the U.S. Congress passed and President Lyndon B. Johnson signed the Wilderness Act of 1964, the "cultural construct" that is the wilderness concept became a "political construct." Wilderness, to the extent that it is a child of the American political system, will remain the "enduring resource" promised by the Act only so long as citizens of the United States understand and support the concept and their elected representatives in Congress express that understanding and support in law. If the concept were to loose support, the law could be changed, and wilderness could be lost. A hallmark of American politics is participation, and there is good reason to believe that the Three Sisters Wilderness and the National Wilderness Preservation System will survive as long as enlightened citizens participate in the process of preserving and managing their unique wilderness heritage.

There are many ways citizens may help meet the wilderness preservation and management challenges at either the local or the national level—or even just during their own wilderness visits. Indeed, a provision of the Wilderness Act of 1964 guarantees citizens the right to be heard in the processes of establishing and managing wilderness, and both the current boundaries and the management policies of the Three Sisters Wilderness reflect citizen involvement.

Among the roles private citizens have played and will continue to play in the management of the Three Sisters Wilderness are serving on wilderness user focus groups, serving in the wilderness as volunteer wilderness rangers and wilderness information specialists, and serving with other organizations who help care for the wilderness. During 1992 and 1993, a Wilderness Strategies Focus Group of 26 wilderness advocates, users, and permittees worked with Deschutes and Willamette national forest wilderness managers to recommend actions that would reduce recreational impacts on the Mt. Jefferson, Mt. Washington, and Three Sisters wildernesses. As a result of this group's recommendations regarding such important issues as solitude and campsite degradation, new regulations—including those on campfire bans, designated campsites, and limited entry areas imposed in the Three Sisters Wilderness in 1995—and other impact reduction measures were put in effect.

As wilderness budgets have declined, volunteer wilderness rangers and wilderness information specialists—as previously described in this chapter—have augmented the dwindling ranks of wilderness rangers employed to serve the public in the wilderness. Still other volunteers affiliated with the Pacific Crest Trail Association and wilderness user groups help maintain trails and rehabilitate impacted areas.

At the national level, private citizens may join wilderness preservation groups such as the Wilderness Society and the Sierra Club to keep informed on wilderness issues and to urge their senators and congressmen to support wilderness preservation legislation and wilderness management funding.

And, at the personal level, all wilderness visitors can take responsibility for their own actions and influencing others' actions in wilderness by practicing and preaching the Leave-No-Trace practices defined by the National Outdoor Leadership School in Appendix C. Ultimately, in this American democracy, it is up to the people to ensure an enduring resource of wilderness.

Suggested Reading

Hendee, John C., and Chad P. Dawson. *Wilderness Management: Stewardship and Protection of Resources and Values.* 3rd ed., Golden, Colorado: Fulcrum Publishing, 2002. *The definitive wilderness management textbook.*

---

[1] Hendee, 15.

[2] Miller, G. Tyler. *Resource Conservation and Management.* (Belmont, California: Wadsworth Publishing Company, 1990) 49.

[3] Hall, Troy E., and Bo Shelby. "Changes in Use of Three Oregon Wildernesses, 1976-1993. (Corvallis, Oregon: Oregon State University, Department of Forest Resources, June 6, 1995) 13, 18.

[4] Zinser, 643.

[5] U.S. Department of Agriculture, Forest Service, and U.S. Department of the Interior, Bureau of Land Management, National Park Service, and Fish and Wildlife Service. *Wilderness Planning.* (Huson, Montana: Arthur Carhart National Wilderness Training Center, 1995) 1-4.

6 Ibid., 1-5.

7 Ibid.

8 Ibid.

9 Ibid.

10 Stegner, Wallace. "Wilderness Letter." *Marking the Sparrow's Fall: Wallace Stegner's American West.* Page Stegner, ed. (New York: Henry Holt and Company, 1998) 112.

11 Ibid., 114.

12 Miller, 49.

13 Bloedel, Ed. "Managing Wilderness as a Resource: Basic Principles." *Proceedings of the Fourth World Wilderness Congress Symposium on Management of Park and Wilderness Lands* (Estes Park, Colorado, 1987) 5.

14 Merigliano, Linda, and Tom Kovalicky. "Toward an Enduring Wilderness Resource." *Journal of Forestry* (February 1993) 16.

15 *Wilderness Planning*, I-v.

16 Ibid, 2-47.

17 Hendee, 11.

18 Ibid., 183.

19 U.S. Department of Agriculture, Forest Service. *Forest Service Manual* (Title 2300, Chapter 2320 "Wilderness Management") 10-11.

20 Hendee, 183.

21 *Wilderness Planning*, 2-32.

22 Ibid., 2-32 and 2-33.

23 Stankey, George H., David N. Cole, Robert C. Lucas, Margaret E. Petersen, and Sidney S. Frissell. *The Limits of Acceptable Change (LAC) System for Wilderness Planning.* (Ogden, Utah: U.S. Department of Agriculture, Forest Service, Intermountain Forest and Range Experiment Station, 1985) 3.

24 Hendee, 209.

25 Ibid.

26 Ibid.

27 Hansen, Gregory F. "Education, The Key to Preservation." *Managing America's Enduring Resource: A Conference.* (Minneapolis, September 11-14, 1989) 123.

28 Peterson, R. Max. "National Forest Dimensions and Dilemmas." *Issues in Wilderness Management.* Michael Frome, ed. (Boulder, Colorado: Westview Press, 1985).

29 Hansen, 124.

30 Ibid., 125.

31 Nelson, Dan. "Legislating Loneliness." *Continental Divide Trail News* (Fall 1998) 8.

32 "Preserve Trail Access." *The Bulletin* (January 17, 1999) E2.

33 U.S. Department of Agriculture, Forest Service. "Green Lakes Loop Trail and Trailhead Reconstruction Environmental Assessment." (Bend: Deschutes National Forest, March 1999) 5.

34 Sabo, Matt. "Heavy Trail Use Could Lead to Limits by Forest Service." *The Bulletin* (April 16, 1999) A1, A6.

35 Neumann, Loretta, and Kathleen M. Reinberg. "Cultural Resources and Wilderness: The White Hats Versus the White Hats." *Journal of Forestry* (October 1989) 10-16.

36 Throop, Gail. *Historic Buildings in Wilderness: A Search for Compatibilities.* (Portland: U.S. Department of Agriculture, Forest Service, Pacific Northwest Region, 1990) 2.

[37] Neuman, Loretta, and Kathleen Schamel, "Mutual Preservation of Cultural Resources and Wilderness Values." (Portland: Threats to Wilderness Conference, May 5, 1992) 2.

[38] Ibid.

[39] Throop, iv.

[40] Ibid.

[41] *Wilderness Planning, 1-7.*

[42] Leopold, Aldo. *A Sand County Almanac and Sketches Here and There.* (New York: Oxford University Press, Inc., 1949) 224-225.

[43] Gordon, Gregory. "U.S. Sees Dollar Signs in Outdoor Recreation." *The Sunday Oregonian* (August 31, 1997) A1, A19.

[44] Ibid.

THE WILDERNESS ACT OF 1964

Public Law 88-577, 88th Congress, September 3, 1964

AN ACT
To establish a National Wilderness Preservation System for the permanent good of the whole people, and for other purposes.

Be it enacted by the Senate and House of representatives of the United States of America in Congress assembled,

SHORT TITLE

Sec. 1. This Act may be cited as the "Wilderness Act."

WILDERNESS SYSTEM ESTABLISHED
STATEMENT OF POLICY

Sec. 2. (a) In order to assure that an increasing population, accompanied by expanding settlement and growing mechanization, does not occupy and modify, all areas within the United States and its possessions, leaving no lands designated for preservation and protection in their natural condition, it is hereby declared to be the policy of the Congress to secure for the American people of present and future generations the benefits of an enduring resource of wilderness. For this purpose there is hereby established a National Wilderness Preservation System to be composed of federally owned areas designated by Congress as "wilderness areas", and these shall be administered for the use and enjoyment of the American people in such manner as will leave them unimpaired for future use and enjoyment as wilderness, and so as to provide for the protection of these areas, the preservation of their wilderness character, and for the gathering and dissemination of information regarding their use and enjoyment as wilderness; and no Federal lands shall be designated as "wilderness areas" except as provided for in this Act or by a subsequent Act.

(b) The inclusion of an area in the National Wilderness Preservation System notwithstanding, the area shall continue to be managed by the Department and agency having jurisdiction thereover immediately before its inclusion in the National Wilderness Preservation System unless otherwise provided by Act of Congress. No appropriation shall be available for the payment of expenses or salaries for the administration of the National Wilderness Preservation System as a separate unit nor shall any appropriations be available for additional personnel stated as being required solely for the purpose of managing or administering areas solely because they are included within the National Wilderness Preservation System.

DEFINITION OF WILDERNESS

(c) A wilderness, in contrast with those areas where man and his own works dominate the landscape, is hereby recognized as an area where the earth and its community of life are untrammeled by man, where man himself is a visitor who does not remain. An area of wilderness is further defined to mean in this Act an area of undeveloped Federal land retaining its primeval character and influence, without permanent improvements or human habitation, which is protected and managed so as to preserve its natural conditions and which (1) generally appears to have been affected primarily by the forces of nature, with the imprint of man's work substantially unnoticeable; (2) has outstanding opportunities for solitude or a primitive and unconfined type of recreation; (3) has at least five thousand acres of land or is of sufficient size as to make practicable its preservation and use in an unimpaired condition; and (4) may also contain ecological, geological, or other features of scientific, educational, scenic, or historical value.

NATIONAL WILDERNESS PRESERVATION
SYSTEM—EXTENT OF SYSTEM

SEC. 3 (a) All areas within the national forests classified at least 30 days before the effective date of the Act by the Secretary of Agriculture or the Chief of the Forest Service as "wilderness", "wild", or "canoe" are hereby designated as wilderness areas. The Secretary of Agriculture shall—

(1) Within one year after the effective date of this Act, file a map and legal description of each wilderness area with the Interior and Insular Affairs Committees of the United States Senate and House of Representatives, and such descriptions shall have the same force and effect as if included in the Act: *Provided however,* That

correction of clerical and typographical errors in such legal descriptions an maps may be made.

(2) Maintain, available to the public, records pertaining to said wilderness areas, including maps and legal descriptions, copies of regulations governing them, copies of public notices of, and reports submitted to Congress regarding pending additions, eliminations, or modifications. Maps, legal descriptions, and regulations pertaining to wilderness areas within their respective jurisdictions also shall be available to the public and in the offices of regional foresters, national forest supervisors, and forest rangers.

(b) The Secretary of Agriculture shall, within ten years after the enactment of this Act, review, as to its suitability or nonsuitability for preservation as wilderness, each area in the national forests classified on the effective date of this Act by the Secretary of Agriculture or the Chief of the Forest Service as "primitive" and report his finding to the President. The President shall advise the United States Senate and House of Representatives of his recommendations with respect to the designation as "wilderness" or other reclassification of each area on which review has been completed, together with maps and a definition of boundaries. Such advice shall be given with respect to not less than one-third of the areas now classified as "primitive" within three years after the enactment of this Act, not less than two-thirds within seven years after the enactment of this Act, and the remaining areas within ten years after the enactment of this Act. Each recommendation of the President for designation as "wilderness" shall become effective only if so provided by an Act of Congress. Areas classified as "primitive" on the effective date of this Act shall continue to be administered under the rules and regulations affecting such areas on the effective date of this Act until Congress has determined otherwise. Any such area may be increased in size by the President at the time he submits his recommendations to the Congress by not more than five thousand acres with no more than one thousand two hundred and eighty acres of such increase in any one compact unit; if it is proposed to increase the size of any such area by more than five thousand acres or by more than one thousand two hundred and eighty acres in any one compact unit the increase in size shall not become effective until acted upon by Congress. Nothing herein contained shall limit the President in proposing, as part of his recommendations to Congress, the alternation of existing boundaries of primitive areas or recommending the addition of any contiguous area of national forest lands predominantly of wilderness value. Notwithstanding any other provisions of this Act, the Secretary of Agriculture may complete this review and delete such area as may be necessary, but not to exceed seven thousand acres, from the southern tip of the Gore Range-Eagles Nest Primitive Area, Colorado, if the Secretary determines that such action is in the public interest.

(c) Within ten years after the effective date of this Act the Secretary of the Interior shall review every roadless area of five thousand contiguous acres or more in the national parks, monuments and other units of the national park system and every such area of, and every roadless area within, the national wildlife refuges and game ranges, under his jurisdiction on the effective date of this Act and shall report to the President his recommendation as to the suitability or nonsuitability of each such area or island for preservation as wilderness. The President shall advise the President of the Senate and the Speaker of the House of Representatives of his recommendation with respect to the designation as wilderness of each such area or island on which review has been completed, together with a map thereof and a definition of its boundaries. Such advice shall be given with respect to not less than one-third of the areas and islands to be reviewed under this subsection within three years after enactment of this Act, not less than two-thirds within seven years of enactment of this Act, and the remainder within ten years of enactment of this Act. A recommendation to the President for designation as wilderness shall become effective only if so provided by an Act of Congress. Nothing contained herein shall, by implication or otherwise, be construed to lessen the present statutory authority of the Secretary of the Interior with respect to the maintenance of roadless areas within units of the national park system.

(d) (1) The Secretary of Agriculture and the Secretary of the Interior shall, prior to submitting any recommendations to the President with respect to the suitability of any area for preservation as wilderness –

(A) give such public notice of the proposed action as they deem appropriate, including publication in the Federal Register and in a newspaper having general circulation in the area or areas in the vicinity of the affected land;
(B) hold a public hearing or hearings at a location or locations convenient to the areas affected. The hearings shall be announced

through such means as the Federal Register and in newspapers of general circulation in the area: *Provided,* That if the lands involved are in more than one State, at least one hearing shall be held in each State in which a portion of the land lies;

(C) at least thirty days before the date of a hearing advise the Governor of the State and the governing board of each county, or in Alaska the borough, in which the lands are located, and Federal departments and agencies concerned, and invite such officials and Federal agencies to submit their views on the proposed action at the hearing by no later than thirty days following the date of the hearing.

(2) Any views submitted to the appropriate Secretary under the provisions of (1) of this subsection with respect to any area shall be included with any recommendations to the President and to Congress with respect to such area.

(e) Any modification or adjustment of boundaries of any wilderness area shall be recommended by the appropriate Secretary after public notice of such proposal and public hearing or hearings as provided in subsection (d) of this section. The proposed modification or adjustment shall then be recommended with map and description thereof to the President. The President shall advise the United States Senate and the House of Representatives of his recommendations with respect to such modification or adjustment and such recommendation shall become effective only in the same manner as provided for in subsections (b) and (c) of this section.

USE OF WILDERNESS

Sec 4. (a) The purposes of this Act are hereby declared to be within and supplemental to the purposes for which national forests and units of the national park and national wildlife refuge systems are established and administered and—

(1) Nothing in this Act shall be deemed to be in interference with the purpose for which national forests are established as set forth in the Act of June 4, 1897 (30 Stat. 11), and the Multiple Use-Sustained-Yield Act of June 12, 1960 (74 Stat. 215).

(2) Nothing in this Act shall modify the restrictions and provisions of the Shipstead-Nolan Act (Public law 733, Seventy-first Congress,

July 10, 1930; 46 Stat. 1020), the Thye-Blatnick Act (Public Law 733, Eightieth Congress, June 22, 1948; 62 Stat. 568), and the Humphrey-Thye-Blatnick-Anderson Act (Public Law 607, Eighty-fourth Congress, June 22, 1956; 70 Stat. 326), as applying to the Superior National Forest or the regulations of the Secretary of Agriculture.

(3) Nothing in this Act shall modify the statutory authority under which units of the national park system are created. Further, the designation of any area of any park, monument, or other unit of the national park system as a wilderness area pursuant to this Act shall in no manner lower the standards evolved for the use and preservation of such park, monument, or other unit of the national park system in accordance with the Act of August 25, 1916, the statutory authority under which the area was created, or any other Act of Congress which might pertain to or affect such area, including, but not limited to, the Act of June 8, 1906 (34 Stat. 225; 16 U.S.C. 432 et seq.); section 3.2 of the Federal Power Act (16 U.S.C. 796(2)); and the Act of August 21, 1935 (49 Stat. 666; 16 U.S.C. 461 et seq.).

(b) Except as otherwise provided in this Act, each agency administering any area designated as wilderness shall be responsible for preserving the wilderness character of the area and shall so administer such area for such other purposes for which it may have been established as also to preserve its wilderness character. Except as otherwise provided in this Act, wilderness areas shall be devoted to the public purposes of recreational, scenic, scientific, educational, conservation, and historical use.

PROHIBITION OF CERTAIN USES

(c) Except as specifically provided for in this Act, and subject to existing private rights, there shall be no commercial enterprise and no permanent road within any wilderness area designated by the Act and, except as necessary to meet minimum requirements for the administration of the area for the purpose of this Act (including measures required in emergencies involving the health and safety of persons within the area), there shall be no temporary road, no use of motor vehicles, motorized equipment or motorboats, no landing of aircraft, no other form of mechanical transport, and no structure or installation within any such area.

SPECIAL PROVISIONS

(d) The following special provisions are hereby made:

(1) Within wilderness areas designated by this Act the use of aircraft or motorboats, where these uses have already become established, may be permitted to continue subject to such restriction as the Secretary of Agriculture deems desirable. In addition, such measures may be taken as may be necessary in the control of fire, insects, and diseases, subject to such conditions as the Secretary deems desirable.

(2) Nothing in this Act shall prevent within national forest wilderness areas any activity, including prospecting, for the purpose of gathering information about mineral or other resources, if such activity is carried on in a manner compatible with the preservation of the wilderness environment. Furthermore, in accordance with such program as the Secretary of the Interior shall develop and conduct in consultation with the Secretary of Agriculture, such areas shall be surveyed on a planned, recurring basis consistent with the concept of wilderness preservation by the Geological Survey and the Bureau of Mines to determine the mineral values, if any, that may be present; and the results of such surveys shall be made available to the public and submitted to the President and Congress.

(3) Notwithstanding any other provisions of this Act, until midnight December 31, 1983, the United States mining laws and all laws pertaining to mineral leasing shall, to the same extent as applicable prior to the effective date of this Act, extend to those national forest lands designated by this Act as "wilderness areas"; subject, however, to such reasonable regulations governing ingress and egress as may be prescribed by the Secretary of Agriculture consistent with the use of land for mineral location and development and exploration, drilling, and production, and use of land for transmission lines, waterlines, telephone lines, or facilities necessary in exploring, drilling, producing, mining, and processing operations, including where essential the use of mechanized ground or air equipment and restoration as near as practicable of the surface of the land disturbed in performing prospecting, location, and in oil and gas leasing, discovery work, exploration, drilling, and production, as soon as they have served their purpose. Mining locations lying within the boundaries of said wilderness areas shall be held and used solely for mining or processing operations and uses rea-

sonably incident thereto; and hereafter, subject to valid existing rights, all patents issued under the mining laws of the United States affecting national forest lands designated by this Act as wilderness areas shall convey title to the mineral deposits within the claim, together with the right to cut and use so much of the mature timber therefrom as may be needed in the extraction, removal, and benefication of the mineral deposits, if needed timber is not otherwise reasonably available, and if the timber is cut under sound principles of forest management as defined by the national forest rules and regulations, but each such patent shall reserve to the United States all title in or to the surface of the lands and the products thereof, and no use of the surface of the claim or the resources therefrom not reasonably required for carrying on mining or prospecting shall be allowed except as otherwise provided in this Act: *Provided,* That, unless hereafter specifically authorized, no patent within wilderness areas designated by this Act shall issue after December 31, 1983, except for the valid claims existing on or before December 31, 1983. Mining claims located after the effective date of this Act within the boundaries of wilderness areas designated by this Act shall create no rights in excess of those rights which may be patented under the provisions of this subsection. Mineral leases, permits, and licenses covering lands within national forest wilderness areas designated by this Act shall contain such reasonable stipulations as may be prescribed by the Secretary of Agriculture for the protection of the wilderness character of the land consistent with the use of the land for the purposes for which they are leased, permitted, or licensed. Subject to valid rights then existing, effective January 1, 1984, the minerals in lands designated by this Act as wilderness areas are withdrawn from all forms of appropriation under the mining laws and from disposition under all laws pertaining to mineral leasing and all amendments thereto.

(4) Within wilderness areas in the national forests designated by this Act, (1) the President may, within a specific area and in accordance with such regulations as he may deem desirable, authorize prospecting for water resources, the establishment and maintenance of reservoirs, water-conservation works, power projects, transmission lines, and other facilities needed in the public interest, including the road construction and maintenance essential to development and use thereof, upon his determination that such use or uses in the specific area will better serve the interests of the United States and the people thereof than will its denial; and (2) the

grazing of livestock, where established prior to the effective date of this Act, shall be permitted to continue subject to such reasonable regulations as are deemed necessary by the Secretary of Agriculture.

(5) Other provisions of this Act to the contrary notwithstanding, the management of the Boundary Waters Canoe Area, formerly designated as the Superior, Little Indian Sioux, and Caribou Roadless areas, in the Superior National Forest, Minnesota, shall be in accordance with regulations established by the Secretary of Agriculture in accordance with the general purpose of maintaining, without unnecessary restrictions on other uses, including that of timber, the primitive character of the area, particularly in the vicinity of the lakes, streams, and portages: *Provided,* That nothing in this Act shall preclude the continuance within the area of any already established use of motortboats.

(6) Commercial services may be performed within the wilderness areas designated by this Act to the extent necessary for activities which are proper for realizing the recreational or other wilderness purposes of the areas.

(7) Nothing in this Act shall constitute an express or implied claim or denial on the part of the Federal Government as to exemption from State water laws.

(8) Nothing in this Act shall be construed as affecting the jurisdiction or responsibilities of the several States with respect to wildlife and fish in the national forests.

STATE AND PRIVATE LANDS WITHIN WILDERNESS

Sec. 5 (a) In any case where State-owned or privately owned land is completely surrounded by national forest lands within areas designated by this Act as wilderness, such State or private owner shall be given such rights as may be necessary to assure adequate access to such State-owned or privately owned land by such State or private owner and their successors in interest, or the State-owned or privately owned land shall be exchanged for federally owned land in the same State of approximately equal value under authorities available to the Secretary of Agriculture: *Provided, however,* That the United States shall not transfer to a State or a private owner any mineral interests unless the State or private owner relinquishes or causes to be relinquished to the United States the mineral interest in the surrounded land.

(b) In any case where valid mining claims or other valid occupancies are wholly within a designated national forest wilderness area, the Secretary of Agriculture shall, by reasonable regulations consistent with the preservation of the area of wilderness, permit ingress and egress to such surrounded areas by means which have been or are being customarily enjoyed with respect to other such areas similarly situated.

(c) Subject to the appropriation of funds by Congress, the Secretary of Agriculture is authorized to acquire privately owned land within the perimeter of any area designated by this Act as wilderness if (1) the owner concurs in such acquisition or (2) the acquisition is specifically authorized by Congress.

GIFTS AND DONATIONS

Sec. 6 (a) The Secretary of Agriculture may accept gifts or bequests of land within wilderness areas designated by this Act for preservation as wilderness. The Secretary of Agriculture may also accept gifts or bequests of land adjacent to wilderness areas designated by this Act for preservation as wilderness if he has given sixty days advance notice thereof to the President of the Senate and the Speaker of the House of Representatives. Land accepted by the Secretary of Agriculture under this section shall become part of the wilderness area involved. Regulations with regard to any such land may be in accordance with such agreements, consistent with the policy of this Act, as are made at the time of such gift, or such conditions, consistent with such policy, as may be included in, and accepted with, such bequest.

(b) The Secretary of Agriculture or the Secretary of the Interior is authorized to accept private contributions and gifts used to further the purposes of this Act.

ANNUAL REPORTS TO CONGRESS

Sec. 7. At the opening of each session of Congress, the Secretaries of Agriculture and Interior shall jointly report to the President for transmission to Congress on the status of the wilderness system, including a list and descriptions of the areas in the system, regulations in effect, and other pertinent information, together with any recommendations they may care to make.

Appendix B

THREE SISTERS WILDERNESS REGULATIONS

A few regulations, all of which are in the Code of Federal Regulations (CFR), help maintain the Three Sisters Wilderness environment and experience. Unless specifically noted, these regulations are in effect year-round. These regulations (as of 2004) follow.

THE FOLLOWING ARE PROHIBITED

Visitor Permits: Being in the Wilderness without a permit beginning the Friday before Memorial Day through October 31st each year. 36CFR261.57a.

Groups: Entering or being in the Wilderness as part of a group or assemblage of more than 12 people or more than 12 head of stock. 36CFR261.57a.

Fire: Building, attending, maintaining, or using a campfire within a 100-foot slope-distance of any permanent water source, system trail, or shelter. 36CFR261.52a.

Livestock: Hitching, tethering, picketing, or securing any pack or saddle stock within a 200-foot slope-distance of any permanent water source, system trail, or shelter. 36CFR261.58a.

Motorized Equipment/Mechanized Transport: Possessing or using bicycles or wheeled transport and or motorized equipment such as chainsaws (except for wheelchairs). 36CFR261.57h, 261.16a, 261.16b.

Sanitation: Possessing or leaving refuse, debris, or litter in an exposed or unsanitary condition. 36CFR261.11b. Failing to dispose of all garbage or material in a proper manner. 36CFR261.11d.

Dogs: From July 1 through September 30th of each year, possessing a dog not on a leash and under physical control. 36CFR261.58s. *Areas affected are the South Sister Climbers Trail, Moraine Lake/Green Lakes trails and areas, Fall Creek Trail, Broken Top Trail, Soda Creek Trail, Crater Ditch Trail.*

Rehabilitated Sites: Camping or being within areas posted as closed for rehabilitation. 36CFR261.58e.

Trees and Vegetation: Cutting or damaging any live tree or vegetation. 36CFR261.6a.

Firearms: Discharging a firearm within 150 yards of a campsite or occupied area or in any manner or place whereby any person is exposed to injury. 36CFR261.10d.

Storing: Storing equipment, personal property, or supplies within the Wilderness for more that 48 hours. 36CFR261.57f.

SITE SPECIFIC REGULATIONS

Also, parts of the Three Sisters Wilderness are governed by the **special area regulations** listed below.

Limited Entry Area: Entering or being in the Obsidian Area of the Three Sisters Wilderness each year between Friday before Memorial Day through October 31st without a permit obtained from the McKenzie Bridge Ranger Station specifically authorizing entry, *except* for through-hikers on the Pacific Crest Trail who do not camp in the area. 36CFR261.57a.

Designated Campsites: Camping is prohibited except within 15 feet of a designated campsite post in specified areas. 36CFR261.58e. *Areas affected are North Matthieu Lake, South Matthieu Lake, Green Lakes, Moraine Lake, Otter Lake, Erma Bell Lakes.*

Fire Ban: Building, attending, or maintaining a campfire is prohibited within the general area. 36CFR261.52a. *Areas affected are the Obsidian Area, South Matthieu Lake, Green Lakes, Moraine Lake, Otter Lake, and Erma Bell Lakes.*

Camping Setback: No camping within 100-foot slope-distance of permanent water or trail. 36CFR261.58e. *Areas affected are the Obsidian Area, Husband/Eileen Lakes, and Linton Meadows.*

These areas have been affected by heavy use and require additional measures to improve their condition and solitude.

PRINCIPLES OF LEAVE NO TRACE

Since 1965, the National Outdoor Leadership School, Lander, Wyoming, has been developing and teaching practical techniques designed to minimize visitor impacts on wilderness and other back-country environments. These techniques are incorporated into the Leave No Trace Principles, a guide to venturing into the Three Sisters Wilderness—or any other wilderness or backcountry area—and leaving only minimal signs of your visit.

Plan Ahead and Prepare
- Know the regulations and special concerns for the area you'll visit.
- Prepare for extreme weather, hazards, and emergencies.
- Schedule your trip to avoid times of high use.
- Visit in small groups. Split larger parties into groups of 4-6.
- Repackage food to minimize waste.
- Use a map and compass to eliminate the use of marking paint, rock cairns or flagging.

Travel and Camp on Durable Surfaces
- Durable surfaces include established trails and campsites, rock, gravel, dry grasses or snow.
- Protect riparian areas by camping at least 200 feet from lakes and streams.
- Good campsites are found, not made. Altering a site is not necessary.
- In popular areas:
    - Concentrate use on existing trails and campsites.
    - Walk single file in the middle of the trail, even when wet or muddy.
    - Keep campsites small. Focus activity in areas where vegetation is absent.
- In pristine areas:
    - Disperse use to prevent the creation of campsites and trails.
    - Avoid places where impacts are just beginning.

Dispose of Waste Properly

- Pack it in, pack it out. Inspect your campsite and rest areas for trash or spilled foods. Pack out all trash, leftover food, and litter.
- Deposit solid human waste in catholes dug 6 to 8 inches deep at least 200 feet from water, camp, and trails. Cover and disguise the cathole when finished.
- Pack out toilet paper and hygiene products.
- To wash yourself or your dishes, carry water 200 feet away from streams or lakes and use small amounts of biodegradable soap. Scatter strained dishwater.

Leave What You Find

- Preserve the past: examine, but do not touch, cultural or historic structures and artifacts.
- Leave rocks, plants and other natural objects as you find them.
- Avoid introducing or transporting non-native species.
- Do not build structures, furniture, or dig trenches.

Minimize Campfire Impacts

- Campfires can cause lasting impacts to the backcountry. Use a lightweight stove for cooking and enjoy a candle lantern for light.
- Where fires are permitted, use established fire rings, fire pans, or mound fires.
- Keep fires small. Only use sticks from the ground that can be broken by hand.
- Burn all wood and coals to ash, put out campfires completely, then scatter cool ashes.

Respect Wildlife

- Observe wildlife from a distance. Do not follow or approach them.
- Never feed animals. Feeding wildlife damages their health, alters natural behaviors, and exposes them to predators and other dangers.
- Protect wildlife and your food by storing rations and trash securely.
- Control pets at all times, or leave them at home.
- Avoid wildlife during sensitive times: mating, nesting, raising young, or winter.

Be Considerate of Other Visitors

- Respect other visitors and protect the quality of their experience.
- Be courteous. Yield to other users on the trail.
- Step to the downhill side of the trail when encountering pack stock.
- Take breaks and camp away from trails and other visitors.
- Let nature's sounds prevail. Avoid loud voices and noises

ACKNOWLEDGMENTS, BIBLIOGRAPHY, AND CREDITS

I acknowledge and appreciate the assistance of several friends and colleagues without which this effort would not have succeeded to the extent I hope it has. Don Pederson, a retired U.S. Forest Service officer who has known both sides of the Three Sisters Wilderness as a district ranger on the Willamette National Forest and a staff officer on the Deschutes National Forest, read most of the manuscript and made many valuable suggestions. Similar contributions were made by Viviane Simon-Brown, Oregon State University, and Marv Lang, Bend-Fort Rock Ranger District, Deschutes National Forest. Larry Chitwood, Deschutes National Forest geologist, and Pat Joslin, my wife and a Bend-Fort Rock Ranger District botanist, contributed their expertise. Doug Rawson, also of the Deschutes National Forest, provided technical data support, and Steve Sorseth, a Willamette National Forest wilderness staff officer, provided information. My daughters, Amy McLaughlin and Wendy Joslin, solved my computer problems. Much of the credit and none of the blame for the result are due these fine folks.

A search for the magnificent Austin Post photographs which illustrate key concepts in this book was successfully facilitated by Marshall Gannett, U.S. Geological Survey, who directed me toward the helpfulness of Rose Watabe and Judy Martsolf of the GeoData Center, Geophysical Institute, University of Alaska, where this remarkable U.S. Geological Survey photographer's collection is curated. Central Oregon Community College partially supported the project with award of a Program for Excellence in Teaching (PET) grant. Gary Asher and his staff at Maverick Publications, Inc., in Bend, Oregon, did their usual outstanding job of helping me realize my vision for this revision of this book.

The following sources informed the writing of this book. Those quoted directly are cited in the notes at the end of each chapter.

Books and Monographs

Baldwin, Donald Nicholas. *The Quiet Revolution: Grass Roots of Today's Wilderness Preservation Movement.* Boulder: Pruett Publishing Company, 1972.

Benson, Jackson J. *Wallace Stegner: His Life and Work.* New York: Penguin Books USA Inc., 1996.

Bishop, Ellen Morris, and John Eliot Allen. *Hiking Oregon's Geology.* Seattle: The Mountaineers, 1996.

Brogan, Phil F. *Visitor Information Service Book for the Deschutes National Forest.* Bend, Oregon: U.S. Department of Agriculture, Forest Service, Deschutes National Forest, 1969.

Browning, James A., John C. Hendee, and Joe W. Roggenbuck. *103 Wilderness Laws: Milestones and Management Direction in Wilderness Legislation, 1964-1987.* Moscow: University of Idaho, 1988.

Coville, Frederick W. *Forest Growth and Sheep Grazing in the Cascade Mountains of Oregon.* U.S. Department of Agriculture, Division of Forestry, Bulletin No. 15. Washington, D.C.: U.S. Government Printing Office, 1898.

Csuti, Blair, et. al. *Atlas of Oregon Wildlife.* Corvallis: Oregon State University Press, 1997.

Doucette, Joseph E. *Wilderness Visitor Education: Information About Alternative Techniques.* Ogden, Utah: U.S. Department of Agriculture, Forest Service, Intermountain Forest and Range Experiment Station, 1993.

Everhart, William C. *The National Park Service.* New York: Praeger Publishers, Inc., 1972.

Fox, Stephen. *John Muir and His Legacy: The American Conservation Movement.* Boston: Little, Brown and Company, 1981.

Franklin, Jerry F., and C.T. Dyrness. *Natural Vegetation of Oregon and Washington.* Portland: U.S. Department of Agriculture, Forest Service, Pacific Northwest Forest and Range Experiment Station, 1973.

Frome, Michael. *Battle for the Wilderness,* rev. ed. Salt Lake City: The University of Utah Press, 1997.

Frome, Michael, ed. *Issues in Wilderness Management.* Boulder: Westview Press, 1985.

Gallagher, Walter. *The White River National Forest, 1891-1981.* Glenwood Springs, Colorado: U.S. Department of Agriculture, Forest Service, White River National Forest, 1981.

Grubbs, Bruce. *Hiking Oregon's Three Sisters Country.* Helena, Montana: Falcon Press Publications, Inc., 1997.

Hall, Troy E., and Bo Shelby. *Changes in Use of Three Oregon Wildernesses, 1976-1993.* Corvallis: Oregon State University, Department of Forest Resources, June 6, 1995.

Harris, Stephen L. *Fire Mountains of the West: The Cascade and Mono Lake Volcanoes.* Missoula, Montana: Mountain Press Publishing Company, 1988.

Hatton, Raymond R. *High Country of Central Oregon.* Portland: Binford & Mort Publishing, 1987.

Hatton, Raymond R. *Oregon's Sisters Country.* Bend, Oregon: Geographical Books, 1996.

Hatton, Raymond R. *Sisters Country Weather and Climate.* Bend, Oregon: Maverick Publications, Inc., 1994.

Hendee, John C., ed. *The Highest Use of Wilderness.* Moscow, Idaho: College of Forestry, Wildlife, and Range Sciences, 1987.

Hendee, John C., George H. Stankey, and Robert C. Lucas. *Wilderness Management.* 2nd ed. Golden, Colorado: North American Press, 1990.

Hodge, Edwin T. *Mount Multnomah: Ancient Ancestor of the Three Sisters.* Eugene: University of Oregon, 1925.

Ibrahim, Hilmi, and Kathleen A. Cordes. *Outdoor Recreation.* Madison: Brown & Benchmark, Publishers, 1993.

Ireland, Orlin. *Plants of the Three Sisters Region, Oregon Cascades.* Eugene: Museum of Natural History, University of Oregon, 1968.

Ise, John. *Our National Park Policy: A Critical History.* Baltimore: The Johns Hopkins Press, 1961.

Jounson, Daniel M., et. al. *Atlas of Oregon Lakes.* Corvallis: Oregon State University Press, 1985.

Knudson, Douglas M. *Outdoor Recreation.* New York: Macmillan Publishing Co., Inc., 1980,

Kovalchik, Bernard L. *Riparian Zone Associations: Deschutes, Ochoco, Fremont, and Winema National Forests.* Portland: U.S. Department of Agriculture, Forest Service, Pacific Northwest Region, 1987.

Kresek, Ray. *Fire Lookouts of Oregon and Washington.* Fairfield, Washington: Ye Galleon Press, 1985.

Leave No Trace Outdoor Skills and Ethics: Pacific Northwest. Lander, Wyoming: National Outdoor Leadership School, 1994.

Leopold, Aldo. *A Sand County Almanac and Sketches Here and There.* New York: Oxford University Press, 1949.

Magley, Beverley. *National Forest Scenic Byways.* Helena, Montana: Falcon Press Publishing Co., Inc. 1990.

Mathews, Daniel. *Cascade-Olympic Natural History.* Portland: Raven Editions, 1988.

McArthur, Lewis L. *Oregon Geographic Names.* 6th ed. Portland: Oregon Historical Society Press, 1992.

Meine, Curt. *Aldo Leopold: His Life and Work.* Madison: The University of Wisconsin Press, 1988.

Merriam, Lawrence C. *Saving Wilderness in the Oregon Cascades:*

The Story of the Friends of the Three Sisters Wilderness. Eugene, Oregon: Friends of the Three Sisters Wilderness, 1999.

Miller, G. Tyler, Jr. *Resource Conservation and Management.* Belmont, California: Wadsworth Publishing Company, 1990.

Muir, John. *My First Summer in the Sierra.* New York: Houghton Mifflin Company, Inc. 1916.

Nash, Roderick. *Wilderness and the American Mind.* 3rd ed. New Haven and London: Yale University Press, 1982.

Orr, Elizabeth, William N. Orr, and Ewart M. Baldwin. *Geology of Oregon.* 4th ed. Dubuque, Iowa: Kendall/Hunt Publishing Company, 1992.

O'Toole, Randal. *Reforming the Forest Service.* Washington, D.C.: Island Press, 1988.

Outdoor Recreation Resources Review Commission. *Outdoor Recreation for America.* Washington, D.C.: U.S. Government Printing Office, 1962.

Peattie, Donald Culross. *A Natural History of Western Trees.* Boston: Houghton Mifflin Company, 1953.

Pinchot, Gifford. *Breaking New Ground.* New York: Harcourt, Brace, and Co., 1947.

Pojar, Jim, and Andy McKinnon. *Plants of the Pacific Northwest Coast.* Redmond, Washington: Lone Pine Publishing, 1994.

Priest, George R., and Beverly F. Vogt, eds. *Geology and Geothermal Resources of the Central Oregon Cascade Range.* Portland: State of Oregon, Department of Geology and Mineral Industries, 1983.

Rakestraw, Lawrence, and Mary Rakestraw. *History of the Willamette National Forest.* Eugene, Oregon: U.S. Department of Agriculture, Forest Service, Willamette National Forest, 1991.

Richmond, Scott. *Fishing in Oregon's Cascade Lakes.* Scappose, Oregon: Flying Pencil Publications, 1994.

Ross, Robert A., and Henrietta L. Chambers. *Wildflowers of the Western Cascades.* Portland: Timber Press, 1988.

Scahffer, Jeffrey P., and Andy Selters. *The Pacific Crest Trail, Volume 2: Oregon & Washington.* Berkeley, California: Wilderness Press, 1990.

Smoot, Jeff. *Summit Guide to the Cascade Volcanoes.* Evergreen, Colorado: Chockstone Press, Inc., 1992.

Stankey, George H., David N. Cole, Robert C. Lucas, Margaret E. Petersen, and Sidney S. Frissell. *The Limits of Acceptable Change (LAC) System for Wilderness Planning.* Ogden, Utah: U.S. Department of Agriculture, Forest Service, Intermountain Forest and Range Experiment Station, 1985.

Steen, Harold K. *The U.S. Forest Service: A History.* Seattle: University of Washington Press, 1991.

Stegner, Page, ed. *Marking the Sparrow's Fall.* New York: Henry Holt & Company, 1998.

Stegner, Wallace. *Where the Bluebird Sings to the Lemonade Spring.* New York: Random House, 1992.

Sullivan, William L. *Exploring Oregon's Wild Areas.* Seattle: The Mountaineers, 1988.

Sullivan, William L. *100 Hikes in the Central Oregon Cascades.* 2nd ed. Eugene, Oregon: Navillus Press, 1998.

Throop, Gail. *Historic Buildings in Wilderness: A Search for Compatibilities.* Portland: U.S. Department of Agriculture, Forest Service, Pacific Northwest Region, 1990.

Tilton, Buck. *America's Wilderness.* San Francisco: Foghorn Press, 1996.

Turner, Frederick. *Rediscovering America: John Muir in His Time and Ours.* New York: Viking Penguin, Inc., 1985.

Udall, Stewart L. *The Quiet Crisis.* New York: Holt, Rinehart and Winston, 1963.

U.S. Department of Agriculture, Forest Service. *The Principal Laws Relating to Forest Service Activities.* Washington, D.C.: U.S. Government Printing Office, 1974.

U.S. Department of Agriculture, Forest Service, and U.S. Department of the Interior, Bureau of Land Management, National Park Service, and Fish and Wildlife Service. *Wilderness Planning.* Huson, Montana: Arthur Carhart National Wilderness Training Center, 1995.

U.S. Department of Agriculture, Forest Service. *Wilderness Ranger Field Guide.* Huson, Montana: Arthur Carhart National Wilderness Training Center, 1993.

Volland, Leonard R. *Plant Associations of the Central Oregon Pumice Zone.* Portland: U.S. Department of Agriculture, Forest Service, Pacific Northwest Region, 1985.

Ward, Geoffrey. *The West.* Boston: Little, Brown and Company, 1996.

West, Terry L. *Centennial Mini-Histories of the Forest Service.* Washington, D.C.: U.S. Department of Agriculture, Forest Service, 1992.

Whitney, Stephen, *Western Forests.* New York: Alfred A. Knopf, Inc., 1985.

Wilkinson, Charles F., and H. Michael Anderson. *Land and Resource Planning in the National Forests.* Washington, D.C.: Island Press, 1987.

Williams, Howel. *Volcanoes of the Three Sisters Region, Oregon Cascades.* Berkeley and Los Angeles: University of California Press, 1944.

Zinser, Charles I. *Outdoor Recreation: United States National Parks, Forests, and Public Lands.* New York: John Wiley & Sons, Inc., 1995.

Periodicals

"A New Way to Keep It Wild." *Sierra* (March/April 1986) 70-71.

Bradley, James C. "An Army of Wilderness Teachers." *Journal of Forestry* (February 1993) 23.

Brunson, Mark W. "The Changing Role of Wilderness in Ecosystem Management." *International Journal of Wilderness* (September 1995) 12-15.

Burgderfer, Don. "Lower Bridge: Oregon Pioneers' 'Other' Major River Crossing." *Cascades East* (Fall 1997) 22-26.

Carter, Dick. "Maintaining Wildlife Naturalness in Wilderness." *International Journal of Wilderness* (September 1997) 17-21.

Cole, David N. "Ecological Manipulation in Wilderness—An Emerging Management Dilemma." *International Journal of Wilderness* (May 1996) 15-18.

Cole, David N. "Recreation Management Priorities are Misplaced—Allocate More Resources to Low-Use Wilderness." *International Journal of Wilderness* (December 1997) 4-8.

Cole, David N. "Wilderness Recreation Management." *Journal of Forestry* (February 1993) 22-24.

Christiansen, Normal L. "Fire and Wilderness." *International Journal of Wilderness* (September 1995) 30-33.

Cronon, William. "The Trouble with Wilderness." *Environmental History* (January 1996) 7-28

Dombeck, Mike. "A Wilderness Agenda and Legacy for the U.S. Forest Service." *International Journal of Wilderness* (December 1999) 4-5.

Duff, Donald A. "Fish Stocking in U.S. Federal Wilderness Areas—Challenges and Opportunities." *International Journal of Wilderness* (September 1995) 17-19.

Edwards, Mike. "A Short Hike with Bob Marshall." *National Geographic* (May 1985) 664-689.

Hammit, William E., and William M. Rutlin. "Achieved Privacy in Wilderness." *International Journal of Wilderness* (March 1997) 19-24.

Kelson, Aaron R., and Robert J. Lilehoilm. "the Influence of Adjacent Land Activities on Wilderness Resources." *International Journal of Wilderness* March 1997) 25-28.

Matthews, Kathleen R., and Roland A. Knapp. "A Study of High Mountain Lake Fish Stocking Effects in the U.S. Sierra Nevada Wilderness." *International Journal of Wilderness* (April 1999) 24-26.

Merigliano, Linda, and Tom Kovalicky. "Toward an Enduring Wilderness Resource." *Journal of Forestry* (February 1993) 16-17.

Merriam, Lawrence C. "The Irony of the Bob Marshall Wilderness." *Journal of Forest History* (April 1989) 81-87.

Mitchell, Mike. "The Secret of the Lost Cabin." *Cascades East* (Fall 1986) 32-34.

Nash, Roderick. "Path to Preservation." *Wilderness* (Summer 1984) 5-11.

Nelson, Dan. "Legislating Loneliness." *Continental Divide Trail News* (Fall 1998) 8.

Rennicke, Jeff. "A Blank Spot on the Map." *Backpacker* (May 1998) 88-94.

Roth, Dennis. "The National Forests and the Campaign for Wilderness Legislation." *Journal of Forest History* (July 1984) 112-125.

Roush, G. Jon. "The Biggest Threat to Wilderness." *International Journal of Wilderness* (September 1995) 8-11.

Stokes, Jerry. "Wilderness Management Priorities in a Changing Political Environment." *International Journal of Wilderness* (April 1999) 4-8.

Taylor, Edward M. "Recent Volcanism Between Three Fingered Jack and North Sister, Oregon Cascades." *The Ore Bin* (July 1965), 121-147.

Winch, Martin. "Tumalo—Thirsty Land, Part I." *Oregon Historical Quarterly* (Winter 1984) 341-374.

Winch, Martin. "Tumalo—Thirsty Land, Part III." *Oregon Historical Quarterly* (Summer 1985) 153-182.

Worf, Bill. "Trammeling the Wilderness: Clash at the Wildland-Urban Interface." *Inner Voice* (July/August 1994) 1, 5.

Newspapers

Babbitt, Bruce. "Melting Glaciers are Harbingers of a Warming Earth." *The Bulletin* (November 2, 1997) F3.

Bernton, Hal. "Forest Service Scrubs Plan to Curtail Hiking." *The Oregonian* (April 8, 1999) A1, A12.

Bolt, Greg. "Few Willing to Pay for Trailpark Pass." *The Bulletin* (December 14, 1997) B1.

Bolt, Greg. "Forests Turn to Toll Trails." *The Bulletin* (February 10, 1997) A1.

Bolt, Greg. "Permits Follow Wilderness Crowds." *The Bulletin* (April 13, 1995) A1.

"Cattle Hoof it to Pasture." *The Redmond Spokesman* (July 7, 1960) 1.

"Cattle Reach Summer Meadow." *The Redmond Spokesman* (July 21, 1960) 1.

Collins, Sally. "Limits on Access Will Be Last Resort for Forest Service." *The Bulletin* (June 5, 1994) F3.

Gaston, Bob. "Over-use Endangers Wilderness Area." *The Bulletin* (August 27, 1971) A1.

Gregory, Gordon. "U.S. Sees Dollar Signs in Outdoor Recreation." *The Sunday Oregonian* (August 31, 1997) A1, A19.

Joslin, Les. "Informed Hikers Back Trail Passes." *The Bulletin* (December 21, 1997) F2.

Joslin, Les. "Patrolling the Wilds." *The Bulletin* (July 2, 1992) E1-E2.

LaBounty, Michelle. "Deschutes Simplifies Trail Fee." *The Bulletin* (January 5, 1999).

Lynch, Ray. "Witness to Collier's Retreat." *The Register-Guard* (May 6, 1979) D1,2.

Maben, Scott. "Efforts to Name Lake after Area Writer Appear Futile." *The Bulletin* (May 17, 1992) D2.

Maben, Scott. "Glaciers Shrink, But Should Weather Drought." *The Bulletin* (September 3, 1992) B1.

Maben, Scott. "Wilderness Group Nears Agreement." *The Bulletin* (February 5, 1993) A2.

Nielson, Jeff. "Little-Known Lake Created a Big Scare." *The Bulletin* (December 3, 1995) B1.

Sabo, Matt. "Heavy Trail Use Could Lead to Limits by Forest Service." *The Bulletin* (April 16, 1999) A1, A6.

Sabo, Matt. "Second Trail Would Ease Congestion." *The Bulletin* (March 16, 1999) C1.

Witty, Jim. "Deschutes Wilderness Feels Crunch of Increased Usage." *The Bulletin* (October 10, 1999) A1, A10.

Witty, Jim. "Fees Still Making for Unhappy Trails." *The Bulletin* (July 4, 1999) A1.

Documents

Bloedel, Ed. "Managing Wilderness as a Resource: Basic Principles." Estes Park, Colorado: *Fourth World Wilderness Congress Symposium on Management of Park and Wilderness Preserves* (September 1987) 6-15.

Hansen, Gregory F. "Education, The Key to Preservation." Minneapolis, Minnesota: *Managing America's Enduring Resource: A Conference* (September 1989) 123-129.

Kenops, Darrel L., and Jose Cruz. "Wilderness Implementation Schedule." U.S. Department of Agriculture, Forest Service, Willamette and Deschutes National Forests, October 1993.

Lakes of the Deschutes National Forest. Portland: Oregon Department of Fish and Wildlife, no date.

Lakes of the Willamette National Forest. Portland: Oregon Department of Fish and Wildlife, 1981.

Spray, Richard H. "The Gila Wilderness: Boundary Adjustments and Other Hi Jinks 1924 to 1980." Silver City, New Mexico: *Southwest Wilderness Conference* (September 1989).

U.S. Department of Agriculture, Forest Service. *Arthur Carhart National Wilderness Training Center.* Huson, Montana: Arthur Carhart National Wilderness Training Center, no date.

U.S. Department of Agriculture, Forest Service. "Bend-Fort Rock Ranger District Handbook." Bend, Oregon: Deschutes National Forest, 1995.

U.S. Department of Agriculture, Forest Service. "Deschutes National Forest Land and Resource Management Plan." Bend, Oregon: Deschutes National Forest, September 1990.

U.S. Department of Agriculture, Forest Service. "Environmental Statement for Mining Rock Mesa (Three Sisters Wilderness)." Bend, Oregon: Deschutes National Forest, November 18, 1970.

U.S. Department of Agriculture, Forest Service. "Experimental Forests and Ranges, Natural Areas, and Primitive Areas: Regulation L-20." Washington, D.C.: Washington Office, 1929.

U.S. Department of Agriculture, Forest Service. "Forest Service Manual: Title 2300, Chapter 2320 "Wilderness Management." Washington, D.C.: Washington Office.

U.S. Department of Agriculture, Forest Service. *Mountain People of Ancient Times.* Eugene, Oregon: Willamette National Forest, 1998.

U.S. Department of Agriculture, Forest Service. "Recreation Plan, Deschutes National Forest." Bend, Oregon: Deschutes National Forest, March 31, 1926.

U.S. Department of Agriculture, Forest Service. "Forest Recreation Plan." Portland: North Pacific District, January 26, 1926.

U.S. Department of Agriculture, Forest Service. "New Wilderness on the Deschutes National Forest: Oregon Wilderness Act of 1984." Portland: Pacific Northwest Region, October 1984.

U.S. Department of Agriculture, Forest Service. "News Release: Three Sisters Action Adds 32,000 Acres to Oregon Wilderness." Portland: Pacific Northwest Region, 1957.

U.S. Department of Agriculture, Forest Service. *Oregon Skyline Trail Map*. Portland: North Pacific Region, 1931.

U.S. Department of Agriculture, Forest Service. "Report on the Three Sisters Primitive Area." Eugene, Oregon: Willamette National Forest, January 3, 1938.

U.S. Department of Agriculture, Forest Service. "Report on the Three Sisters Primitive Area." Portland: North Pacific Region, October 24, 1935.

Letters and Memoranda

Aufderheide, Robert F., Forest Supervisor, Willamette National Forest, Eugene, Oregon: memorandum of January 6, 1955 "Staff Meeting Held January 5, 1955, to Discuss Three Sisters Wilderness Area."

Cruz, Jose, Forest Supervisor, Deschutes National Forest, Bend, Oregon: memorandum of July 29, 1993 "Focus Group Recommendations."

Folsom, Frank B., Assistant Regional Forester, Pacific Northwest Region, Portland, Oregon: letter of January 21, 1960, to George Van Vechten, Botany Department, Oregon State College, Corvallis, Oregon.

Horton, F.V., Regional Forester, Pacific Northwest Region, Portland, Oregon: memorandum of September 28, 1934 "Memorandum to Forest Supervisors."

Kenops, Darrell L., Forest Supervisor, Willamette National Forest, Eugene, Oregon, and Sally Collins, Forest Supervisor, Deschutes National Forest, Bend, Oregon: memorandum of July 28, 1995 "Prescribed Natural Fire."

Neal, Carl B., Forest Supervisor, Deschutes National Forest, Bend, Oregon: letter of November 19, 1934, to P.A. Thompson, Forest Supervisor, Willamette National Forest.

Pederson, Donald H., Recreation Staff Officer, Deschutes National Forest, Bend, Oregon: memorandum of January 13, 1978 "Coordinated Management of the Three Sisters Wilderness."

Stone, J. Herbert, Regional Forester, Pacific Northwest Region, Portland, Oregon: letter of January 17, 1955 to forest supervisors "U-Classification—Willamette, Three Sisters Wilderness Area."

Thompson, P.A., Forest Supervisor, Willamette National Forest, Eugene, Oregon: letter of November 23, 1934, to Carl B. Neal, Forest Supervisor, Deschutes National Forest.

Photographs

Photographs and illustrations, other than those taken or prepared by the author: page 5, Muir courtesy of the *Dictionary of American Portraits*, published by Dover Publications, Inc., in 1967, and Pinchot courtesy of the U.S. Forest Service; page 7, Leopold, John D. Guthrie, U.S. Forest Service, and Carhart, U.S. Forest Service, courtesy of the Forest History Society, Durham, North Carolina; page 10, U.S. Forest Service; page 13, U.S. Forest Service, courtesy of the Forest History Society; page 16, U.S. Forest Service; page 18, Forest History Society; page 20, Leland J. Prater, U.S. Forest Service; page 28, Joyce Milner; page 33, Austin Post, U.S. Geological Survey; page 39, Austin Post, U.S. Geological Survey; page 40, Rob Phillips; page 42, U.S. Forest Service (top), Austin Post, U.S. Geological Survey (bottom); page 43, Rob Phillips; page 45, Bob Jensen, U.S. Forest Service; page 68, Mrs. Walt McCoin, courtesy of Ray Hatton; page 69, U.S. Forest Service; page 73, U.S. Forest Service; page 74, Chris Sabo, U.S. Forest Service; page 76, R.A. Elliott, U.S. Forest Service; page 92, Pat Joslin; page 97, U.S. Forest Service; page 101, Tom Iraci, U.S. Forest Service; page 111, Chris Sabo, U.S. Forest Service; page 123, Pat Joslin; page 125, Barbara Merlin, U.S. Forest Service.

INDEX

Italicized page numbers indicate a photograph or map.

otters 60
Pacific Crest National Scenic
  Trail 74
Pacific Crest Trail 71, 74-75, 97
Pacific Crest Trail Association 130
Pacific High 33
Pacific Ocean 32
Pacific Railroad Survey of 1855
  62
Pacific yew 84
Packsaddle Mountain 51, 53, 76
Packwood, Senator Bob 22, 78
Park Creek 23
Park Meadow 23, 67
Peterson, Assistant Secretary of
  Agriculture E.L. 15
Phantom Lake 54
pika 49
Pinchot, Gifford,
  Chief Forester 4-6, 9
pinemat manzanita 54
Plainview 65, 67
plate tectonics 29
Pole Creek 65, 67
policy of nondegradation 91
ponderosa pine 49, 54
Pooler, Frank C.W., District
  Forester 8
Porky Lake 52
prescribed natural fire (PNF)
  108-109
preservationists 3
principles of wilderness
  management 103-121
Prouty Glacier 37, 41
Proxy Creek 58
Proxy Falls *57*, 58, 75, 98, 111
Proxy Point 55, 58
pumice grapefern 48, 85
Puppy Lake 53
Pyramid Mountain 56

—Q - R—

Quaking Aspen Swamp 60
Rainbow Creek 23

Rainbow Falls 23
Reagan, President Ronald 71
Rebel Creek 30, 58, 75
Rebel Rock 56, 76, 117
recreation carrying capacity 92
Recreation Fee Demonstration
  Program 127-129
Red Hill 51
Regulation U-1 18
Renfrew Glacier 41
resource 83
resource, public property 86
resource, wilderness 86
Roadless Area Review and
  Evaluation (RARE I) 21-22,
  (RARE II) 22
Robert Aufderheide Memorial
  Drive 75
Rock Mesa 37-*39*, 40, 55,
  70-71, 120
Rock Rim Lake 53
Roosevelt, President Theodore 4

—S—

Salem, Oregon 62
Santiam National Forest 63
Save French Pete Committee 22
Sawtooth Ridge 56, 60
Saylor, Representative John P. 17
Scott Pass 62
Scott Trail 62
Scott, Felix and Marion 62
Separation Creek 32, 55, 58
Sierra Club 4, 98, 130
Sierra Nevada 3
Silcox, Ferdinand A., Chief of the
  Forest Service 11, 13
Sisters Mirror Lake 52, 97
Sisters, Oregon 47, 85, 89
Skinner Glacier 41
Skyline Road 72
Skyline Trail 72
Smokey Bear 99, 109
Snowshoe Lake 52
Soda Creek 38, 44, 47, 64

Other Books from Wilderness Associates...

WALT PERRY
An Early-Day Forest Ranger in New Mexico and Oregon

By Walter J. Perry, edited by Les Joslin

Walt Perry (1873-1959) lived an amazing life. After working at many jobs—most notably mining and logging in Mexico—he found his "real life's work" in the U.S. Forest Service. He served on national forests in New Mexico and Oregon, from 1910 to 1936, as a forest ranger and timber manager. A graduate of the "school of hard knocks," he rose through the ranks to become a senior member of the Society of American Foresters and a respected member of the forestry profession. Along the way, he served with many of the Forest Service's best. He also made major contributions to North American anthropology and was an accomplished naturalist, writer, and poet.

1999, 205 pages, 32 historic photos, ISBN 0-9647167-2-0, $15.95 postpaid

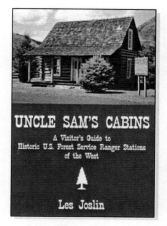

UNCLE SAM'S CABINS
A Vistor's Guide to Historic U.S. Forest Service Ranger Stations of the West

By Les Joslin

Uncle Sam's Cabins is a step back in time to seventy-five historic U.S Forest Service ranger stations throughout the West—stations from which early-day forest rangers patrolled and protected America's magnificent national forests. Some of these sites remain in use as ranger or guard stations. Others are preserved and interpreted by the Forest Service. All are fascinating. Access information is provided for each in this first guidebook to historic Forest Service ranger stations.

1995, 252 pages, 130 photographs, 7 maps, ISBN 0-9647167-1-2, $15.95 postpaid

Order either or both of these books from
Wilderness Associates
P.O. Box 5822, Bend, Oregon 97708

Wilderness Associates is a private partner in the preservation and interpretatin of America's National Forest System and National Wilderness Preservation System heritage.